FINANCIAL CONGLOMERATES

Financial Conglomerates

New Rules for New Players?

Edited by

Lutgart Van den Berghe

Erasmus Finance and Insurance Centre,
Erasmus University Rotterdam, The Netherlands
and The Vlerick School of Management,
University of Ghent, Belgium

Research sponsored by The Levob Foundation
&
The Insurance Science Foundation

KLUWER ACADEMIC PUBLISHERS

DORDRECHT / BOSTON / LONDON

Library of Congress Cataloging-in-Publication Data

```
Financial conglomerates : new rules for new players? / edited by
  Lutgart Van den Berghe.
       p.    cm.
  Includes index.
  ISBN 0-7923-3753-0 (hardbound : alk. paper)
  1. Financial institutions--Europe.  2. Conglomerate corporations-
-Europe.    I. Berghe, L. van den (Lutgart), 1951-
HG186.A2F54   1995
332.1'6--dc20                                           95-36033
```

ISBN 0-7923-3753-0 (HB)

Published by Kluwer Academic Publishers,
P.O. Box 17, 3300 AA Dordrecht, The Netherlands.

Kluwer Academic Publishers incorporates
the publishing programmes of
D. Reidel, Martinus Nijhoff, Dr W. Junk and MTP Press.

Sold and distributed in the U.S.A. and Canada
by Kluwer Academic Publishers,
101 Philip Drive, Norwell, MA 02061, U.S.A.

In all other countries, sold and distributed
by Kluwer Academic Publishers Group,
P.O. Box 322, 3300 AH Dordrecht, The Netherlands.

Printed on acid-free paper

Printed in the Netherlands

Contents

Foreword xi

1.   **Defining financial conglomerates**
      Combining economic and legal approaches 1

1.1.   The essential elements that constitute a financial
       conglomerate 2
1.2.   Defining a group of enterprises 2
1.2.1.   Participation versus investment 3
1.2.2.   Direct versus indirect participations 5
1.2.3.   Ownership versus control 6
1.2.4.   Economic versus legal integration 7
1.3.   Defining financial institutions and financial activities 9
1.4.   What distinguishes a financial conglomerate from a financial
       institution? 11
1.5.   Complementarity between the activities and institutions
       involved 12
1.6.   A financial conglomerate is not really a conglomerate in the
       economic sense of the word 14
       Appendix 1.A. Relevant definitions 16
A.1.   Defining a group 16
A.2.   Defining a daughter company or subsidiary 17
A.3.   Defining a participation 17
A.4.   Defining an associated or related enterprise 17
A.5.   Defining a financial conglomerate 18

2.   **Defining financial conglomerates; Discussion** 21
2.1.   Discussion by dr. A.J. Vermaat 21
2.1.1.   One or more definitions ? 21
2.1.2.   General theory of conglomerates 21
2.1.3.   The term "financial conglomerate" in the context of supervision 22
2.1.4.   An attempt to a simple typology 23
2.2.   Discussion by Drs. J.H. Holsboer 26
2.2.1.   Definition 26
2.2.2.   Level playing field 26

2.2.3. Participation versus investment and the 'droit de suite' 26
2.3.   Discussion by dr. K.W. Knauth 27
2.3.2. What are the essential elements that constitute a financial
        conglomerate? 27
2.3.2. Defining a group of enterprises 29
2.4.   Discussion by P. Pearson 29
2.4.1. Seeking a legal definition of a financial conglomerate 29
2.4.2. The relevant relationship between the undertakings ("group") 31
2.4.3. The relevant activities and undertakings ("supervised companies
        providing financial services") 33
2.4.4. The specific composition of the "group" (activities consist "largely,
        though not necessarily wholly of financial services of at least two
        different sectors") 34
2.5.   The case Norway by S. Simonsen 36
2.5.1. Background 36
2.5.2. Definition of a financial group 38
2.5.3. Organisation 40
2.5.4. Concurrent positions in boards 40
2.5.5. Transactions between companies (enterprises) in a financial group 41
        Appendix 2.A. 43
A.1.   Financial institutions 43
A.1.1. Ownership structure, etc. 43
A.1.2. General rules for business 47
A.2.   Financial groups 47
A.2.1. Licence 48
A.2.2. Organisational set-up 49
A.2.3. Transactions and consolidation 50

3.   **Application of the most relevant definitions
        to the relational database** 53
3.1.   The collection of the data 54
3.2.   The results 56
3.2.1. Defining the type and number of financial conglomerates 56
3.2.2. Economic impact of the financial conglomerates: some estimations 61

4.   **Financial conglomerates; Risks?** 69
4.1.   What are the potential risks in relation to financial
        conglomerates ? 69

4.1.1.	The risks of instability and insolvency	69
4.1.2.	The risk of non-transparency	71
4.1.3.	The risk of infringing the free competition and the rights of the consumer	71
4.2.	The supervision of financial conglomerates	72

5. Solvency regulations for financial conglomerates 77

5.1.	Calculation of the required level of solvency for credit institutions and for insurance companies	78
5.1.1.	Credit Institutions	78
5.1.2.	Insurance Companies	79
5.2.	Calculation of the solvency fund for credit institutions and insurance companies	81
5.2.1.	Credit institutions	81
5.2.2.	Insurance companies	81
5.3.	Other elements that must guarantee the stability and confidence in the financial and insurance sector	83
5.3.1.	Credit institutions	83
5.3.2.	Insurance companies	83
5.4.	Philosophy behind the solvency requirements for credit institutions and insurance companies	84
5.4.1.	General observations	84
5.4.2.	Philosophy behind the solvency regulations	86
	Appendix 5.A. Credit institutions	89
A.1.	What is the minimum level of solvency?	89
A.1.1.	Minimum level of solvency from 1-1-1993 until 1-1-1994	89
A.1.2.	Kind of risk	90
A.1.3.	Kind of risk only for OBS activities	90
A.1.4.	Weighted Assets	90
A.1.5.	Weighted Off-Balance-Sheet elements	91
A.1.6.	Minimum level of solvency from 1-1-1994 until 1-7-95 (including large risk)	91
A.2.	Components of solvency	92
A.3.	Risk weighting factors	93
	Appendix 5.B. Insurance companies	97
B.1.	What is the minimum level of solvency	97

B.1.1.   Non-life insurance 97
B.1.2.   Minimum guarantee fund 97
B.1.3.   Solvency level based on premiums (Xt-1) 97
B.1.4.   Solvency level based on average claims (Zt-1) 98
B.1.5.   Life insurance 99
B.1.6.   Minimum guarantee fund 99
B.1.7.   Solvency level based on mathematical reserves and/or capital under
         risk 99
B.2.   Components of solvency 101
B.2.1.   Non-life insurance 101
B.2.2.   Life insurance 102
B.3.   List of symbols 103
         Appendix 5.C. Comparison of own funds 105

**6.   Research into the possibility of a global ap-
         proach for the calculation of the solvency
         requirements of financial conglomerates** 107
6.1.   Some theoretical remarks 107
6.1.1.   Do financial conglomerates lead to a decreasing or to an increasing
         entrepreneurial risk? 108
6.1.2.   Does the solvency requirements of insurance companies need an
         upgrading to take also the "asset" risks into account ? 108
6.2.   Simulations of the combined solvency 109
6.2.1.   The calculation of the required solvency level for insurers on the basis
         of the banking rules 110
6.2.2.   The calculation of the solvency fund for insurers on the basis of the
         banking rules 111
6.2.3.   Analysis of the simulation results 111
6.3.   Analysis of the need for an actualisation of the minimum
         solvency requirements 113
         **Appendix 6.A. Theoretical problems in the applica-
         tion of the banking rules to insurance companies** 115
A.1.   Definition of the solvency needed: the weighting factors 115
         Appendix 6.B. Simulation exercises 117
B.1.   Calculation of the solvency required according to the
         banking directives 117
B.2.   Combining solvency requirements according to insurance
         and banking rules 119

Appendix 6.C. Correction: minimum solvency levels 122
C.1. Correction on the European level 122
C.2. Corrections for the Dutch market 123

7. Financial conglomerates, solvency and risks 125
7.1. Discussion by S. Simonsen 125
7.1.1. Solidity requirements 125
7.1.2. Consolidation 127
7.1.3. Supervision 127
7.2. Discussion by Ø. Løining 128
7.3. Risk-based capital in the United States, discussion by J. Roos 133
7.3.1. Introduction 133
7.3.2. Risk-based capital ratio 133
7.3.3. The ACL RBC of life insurers 134
7.3.4. The ACL RBC of property/casualty insurers 137
7.4. Discussion by drs. J.H. Holsboer 139
7.4.1. Consolidated versus solo-plus supervision 139
7.4.2. Development of supervisory rules in relation to 'incidents' 139
7.4.3. Applying the BIS-ratio to insurance companies 140
7.4.4. Revaluation reserves of insurance companies as Tier 2 capital 140
7.4.5. Risk based capital solvency regulations 141
7.4.6. Role of rating agencies 141
7.5. Discussion by dr. K.W. Knauth 142
7.5.1. Solvency regulations for financial conglomerates 142
7.5.2. The risk of contagion 142
7.5.3. Double gearing 143
7.5.4. Research into the possibility of a global approach for the calculation of the solvency requirements of financial conglomerates 143
7.6. Discussion by P. Pearson 145
7.6.1. Solvency Regulations for financial conglomerates 145
7.6.2. Minimum guarantee funds 146
Appendix 7.A. Thresholds and minimum guarantee funds 148

8.   **Why financial conglomerates?
Strategic Issues** 149

8.1.   What is the reasoning behind the formation of a financial
conglomerate ? 149

8.2.   Financial conglomerates: new wave strategic thinking? 150

8.3.   Strategy at the limits of the possible: the management
recipe of the nineties 151

8.4.   Strategy at the limits of the possible goes further than
internal creativity 152

8.5.   The formation of financial conglomerates can be a strategy
at the limits of the possible 153

8.5.1.   Internal creativity at the limits of the possible 153

8.5.2.   External (and internal) creativity at the limits of the possible 154

8.6.   Conclusions 155

9.   **Summary and Conclusions** 157

9.1.   Part I - Definitions 157

9.1.1.   What are the essential elements that constitute a financial
conglomerate ? 157

9.1.2.   Defining a group of enterprises 158

9.1.3.   Defining different kinds of financial institutions 161

9.1.4.   Applying the definitions in practice 163

9.2.   Part II - Regulating financial conglomerates 168

9.2.1.   Risks in relation to financial conglomerates 168

9.2.2.   Supervision of financial conglomerates 169

9.2.3.   Solvency regulations for financial conglomerates 169

9.2.4.   The possibility of a global approach for the calculation of the solvency
requirements of financial conglomerates 170

9.2.5.   Discussion on risks and solvency 171

9.3.   Part III - Strategic issues 172

9.3.1.   Strategic issues 172

9.3.2.   Basis statements to be tested in further research 172

Index 175

Foreword

The last couple of years, financial conglomerates have been established all over Europe. This horizontal diversification has not only attracted a great deal of attention in the banking and insurance sector but has also alarmed the supervisory authorities and the European Commission. Although the benefits of financial conglomerates are straightforward, it is clear that quite a number of potential risks can not be ignored.

Since the phenomenon of "financial conglomeration" is rather new, the regulators do not possess a great deal of objective, scientific reference bases on which to construct the necessary regulations. Moreover the complexities and specific characteristics of the financial conglomerates do not permit a simple extrapolation of the rules for industrial conglomerates. Even the extrapolation of banking regulations to insurance groups and vice versa poses a lot of difficult questions.

These observations lie at the origin of the research carried out at the Erasmus Finance and Insurance Centre (EFIC at the Erasmus University in Rotterdam), in collaboration with the Impulse Centre for Financial Services and Insurance (ALEA at the Vlerick School of Management of the University of Ghent).

To confront the research results with the expertise of the business world and the supervisory authorities a workshop was organised in Rotterdam (1994). This publication is partly based on these research results and the workshop discussions. Three main blocs can be distinguished:

- the definition of financial conglomerates;
- the potential risks and the regulatory aspects;
- the strategic issues.

Part I gives a broad overview of possible definitions and discusses the usefulness of them, as well from an economic, a regulatory as a strategic point of view. Moreover an attempt is made to apply some of those definitions to have an idea of the importance of this "financial conglomeration" trend.

Part II gives an overview of potential risks that can evolve through the establishment of financial conglomerates. Also potential topics for regulation are discussed. Special interest is devoted to the comparison of the solvency regulations for banks and insurance companies and an attempt is made to adapt the banking rules to insurance companies. These "solvency" aspects are discussed at length by the business sectors involved as well as by their supervisors.

Part III gives insight into the strategic issues explaining the creation of financial conglomerates.

The publication is concluded by a synthesis and some ideas for further research.

The realisation of this book was only possible thanks to the help of many persons. Different authors and discussants co-operated in this initiative. Their names are mentioned in the table of contents. The hard task of integrating the many discussion topics has been carried out by Frans Dooren. The editing job has been a joint effort of many collaborators, whom I want to thank personally: Xavier Baeten, Frans Dooren, Janneke Roos, Janneke Suijker, Jaap van der Veen, Annick Vervaet and my colleague Alfred Oosenbrug.

Let us hope that this publication can shed some light on the complex subject of financial conglomerates. The more we analyse the topic the more we get convinced that it is such a complicated phenomenon that further research is needed in order to have a clear insight in the many aspects involved.

Prof. dr. L. Van den Berghe

1. Defining financial conglomerates

Combining economic and legal approaches

L.A.A. Van den Berghe
Erasmus Finance & Insurance Centre (NL)
De Vlerick School voor Management (B)

The formation of financial conglomerates and the increasing interface between insurance companies, banks and other financial institutions have attracted a great deal of attention from the business sectors involved as well as from the regulatory authorities. The (presumed) risks of this diversification have been under discussion and different circles suggested that some extra or new regulations are necessary.
Before being able to make an analysis of the potential risks involved and the necessary supervision, one must clearly understand the concepts of "financial conglomerates" and of "all finance diversification".

The Erasmus Finance & Insurance Centre has undertaken quite an exhaustive analysis of the most relevant literature to make an inventory of the concepts that could be used to define and analyse the "financial conglomerates"[1]. Comparison of all relevant information led to a set of standard components defining a financial conglomerate. Not only legal texts and documents but also economic analyses and reports have been used in this respect.
Complementary to this analysis a large scale relational database has been set up to test the different definitions and their economic impact[2].

[1]   A great deal of the data collection has been carried out by Janneke Roos, research assistant at the Erasmus Finance and Insurance Centre. Helpful assistance has also been given by Margo van Felius, former student-assistant.
[2]   This research was carried out under the responsibility of Kurt Verweire, research assistant at The Vlerick School of Management as well as at the Erasmus Insurance Centre. Valuable collaboration was provided by Jaap van der Veen (for the database) and by Marco Scheffers (for the data analysis).

1.1. THE ESSENTIAL ELEMENTS THAT CONSTITUTE A FINANCIAL CONGLOMERATE

From the research carried out by the Comité Européen des Assurances[3] it became clear that a "legal" definition of financial conglomerates is lacking (only 1 out of 13 European countries - Spain - mentioned that they had a definition of what has to be considered as a financial conglomerate (see appendix 1.A.)).

From our analysis at the Erasmus University, we found that quite a number of definitions can be used to describe what essential elements constitute a financial conglomerate. We used some 50 legal documents and reports (see bibliographic references). An overview of some relevant definitions can be found in appendix 1.A. This paper focuses on the components defining a financial conglomerate and on the potential questions to be discussed when defining this concept.

The essential elements, prevailing in most of the definitions, are :

-   it relates to a group of enterprises; therefore the concept of group and holding will have to be defined further (see paragraph 1.2.);
-   it is a combination of different kinds of financial institutions or of different types of financial services or activities;
-   consequently one has to define further what a financial institution and a financial service are and what types of institutions and services can be involved in defining a financial conglomerate (see paragraph 1.3.);
-   being different is often linked to the concept of being subject to different types of supervisory rules (see paragraph 1.4.);
-   the difference in the services offered is sometimes limited to the extent that there must exist a certain degree of complementarity (see paragraph 1.5.).

1.2. DEFINING A GROUP OF ENTERPRISES

The relevant literature to define the concept of a group or holding is quite substantial. Definitions often differ according to the type of the user(s) or the use made of it. For instance, the viewpoint of a shareholder might be significantly different from that of a creditor or a supervisor.[4]

To define a group one has to analyse in greater detail the most relevant components distinguishing relationships that can be seen as forming a group company from those that cannot be defined in this way. These basic components are:

---

[3]   CEA (1993).
[4]   Kredietbank (1994).

- participation versus investment;
- direct versus indirect participations;
- ownership versus control;
- economic versus legal integration.

1.2.1. PARTICIPATION VERSUS INVESTMENT

In the strict legal sense of the term, a group refers to a legal structure that combines a set of companies.

The first question which has to be tackled in analysing this definition is:

> to what extent can the ownership of a stake in another company be seen as a criterion to be included as a group company?

In other words: how large must the share in the capital of a corporation be, before it can be identified as a group company?

There is no unanimity as to the answer to this question. Different types of regulatory prescripitons use different sets of definitions. Some examples in this respect are the following:

defining "qualifying holdings" and "significant influence":
- the directives concerning the freedom of services for financial institutions define qualifying holdings as direct or indirect holdings of at least 10% of the shares or voting rights or as holdings giving the possibility of influencing the management of the enterprise in question (OJEC 89/646/EC, 92/49/EC, 92/96/EC, 93/22/EC);
- the CEA-analysis of financial conglomerates (1993) shows rather confusing results in their overview of national legislation on financial conglomerates; for Belgium they refer to the regulation of financial shareholdings in the insurance law of 1975 and to the regulation of public purchase offers and quote that a "qualified holding" is a holding of less than 10%[5] of the capital or voting rights; in Germany on the contrary, it seems that a qualified holding means a participation that is sufficient to block certain decisions, which is at least 25%;
- a significant influence is "assumed" to exist in Belgium[6], if the company possesses at least 20% of the voting rights;
- the notification duties in relation to the acquisition, increase or decrease of holdings in another corporation, are set out according to the relative importance of these holdings; the thresholds used are (> or =) 20, 33 and 50% of the voting rights or shares (Benink - 1993);

---

[5] To our opinion, this is a mistake.
[6] KB 06.03.1990 (BS 27.03.1990), changed by KB 30.12.1991 (BS 31.12.1991) and KB 03.12.1993 (BS 23.12.1993).

defining "participations":
- the EC tax legislation defines a participation as a combination of a minimal ownership and some form of "lasting" relationship and influence; no clear distinction is made between a participation and an investment;
  the Dutch regulation of company taxes defines a participation as a holding in a company of at least 5% of the nominal paid-up capital. To benefit from the participation exemption rule, this "participation" cannot be owned for pure investment purposes (Leemreis - 1994); a holding of more than 25% of the capital that has a pure investment purpose can eventually be considered as a participation (and benefit from the tax exemption);
- for accounting purposes a distinction is also made between participations (which are considered as fixed financial assets) and investments (which do not have this "fixed" character, and which are classified as "current assets");
- in Belgium a share of at least 10% of the capital can lead to a participation only in as far as this share has a permanent character (a lasting relationship) and leads to some form of influence upon the management of the enterprise involved;
- there is a legal assumption that a participation exists if a company or group owns directly or indirectly a minimum of 20% of the capital of another enterprise; this assumption is not retained if it is clear that the basic premises that distinguish a participation from an investment are not fulfilled (Moret & Limperg - 1985);
  this is also in accordance with the EC-legislation of 1978 (OJEC 78/660/EC) which laid down the limits to define a participation (maximum limit for the assumption was 20%);
- in 1983, the consolidation of credit institutions referred to a participation if a firm owned directly or indirectly 25% or more of the capital of another institution (OJEC 83/350/EC); in the 7th directive on company accounts, the threshold for consolidation was reduced from 25% to 20% of the capital or the voting rights (OJEC 92/30/EC on the consolidation of credit institutions); the consolidation methods will differ according to the type of participation :
  * more than 50% of the capital (full consolidation);
  * 50% or less but with effective control (full (preferred) or proportional consolidation method);
  * 50% or less but without effective control (agreement could eventually be reached to use a proportional consolidation);
- in the BCCI-directive (COM(93), 363 - 1993) a participation means the owner-ship, direct or indirect, of 20% or more of the voting rights or capital of an enterprise;
- the analysis of financial conglomerates by the CEA (1993) started from participations of at least 10%.

In our statistical research we analysed four levels of participation:

- more than 50% or majority of the stocks; this is often seen as a "mother/daughter - relationship" (see appendix 1.A.);
- between 20 and 50%, what could be seen as a "substantial stake"; this can be classified as a "qualifying holding" or a "participation" (for more details see appendix 1.A.);
- between 5 and 20%, what could be interpreted as a "minor stake";
- less than 5% what can be defined more as an investment than as a participation.

The consequences of these differences in definition will be examined in greater detail in chapter 3.

1.2.2. DIRECT VERSUS INDIRECT PARTICIPATIONS

Another complicating factor in defining the members of a group or conglomerate relates to the question:

should the analysis only be based on the direct participations, or to what extent should indirect relationships (through intra-group shareholding constructions) have to be taken into consideration?

Most definitions use direct as well as indirect participations. If indirect relationships have to be taken into account, the question remains to what degree and by which method these indirect participations should be calculated. Is a pure mathematical calculation possible?

To clarify this discussion, the following analysis can be made[7] :

- A has a 40% participation in B and C:
  if the majority criterion is used and the calculation is limited to the direct participations, then neither A, nor B or C belong to a group;
  if, on the contrary, the indirect participations are also taken into account, then A & C can form a group, as far as the total participation is the criterion (A owns C for 40% + (40%x40%) or for 56%);
  it is not clear from these statistics whether A controls C (and/or B); therefore the distinction between participation and control has to be made (see paragraph 1.2.3.);
- A owns 80% of B; B owns 60% of C :
  in all cases it is clear that all three companies form a group and that A is the parent of B (directly = daughter) and of C (indirectly = grandchild), even although A only has an indirect participation in C of 48% (80% x 60%).

---

[7]   This analysis is based upon Moret & Limperg (1985).

According to Moret & Limperg (1985), control is an essential element in analysing the indirect participations.

1.2.3. OWNERSHIP VERSUS CONTROL

Depending upon the legal structure of the company, its type(s) of shares[8], the dispersion of the ownership, the existence of a syndicate agreement between important shareholders etc., it is clear that the percentage of stock owned by another (group) company is not the complete answer to the question whether the companies can be seen as a group or not. In other words, a substantial share or even a minority share can lead to a majority in votes or to a controlling position.

The measurement of the group structure, based on the control criterion is much more difficult to analyse[9] than the definition based on the participation in the stock capital. There is not enough externally available information in this respect.

An indirect measure which can be used is the division of votes in the meeting of shareholders (control is then defined as majority of the votes represented at the meeting) or the companies represented in the board (names of persons representing the controlling shareholders; control is then defined as the possibility to nominate the majority of directors). A group can also be defined on the base of more qualitative indicators, such as the "unity of organisation", the "co-ordinated management" or the "degree of decisive power (to orient the strategy and the business policy)".

In the first phase of our research we have not included this definition in the analysis. The main reason therefore is the lack of reliable data, rather than the definition not being relevant.
As far as it becomes possible to collect the necessary data, we would be interested in completing our relational database, so that we would be able to upgrade and check the reliability of our database.

It is, however, not yet clear to what extent the definition of a financial conglomerate must be based on the criterion of participation or on the criterion of control.

Some definitions consider the control measure as the only relevant criterion in this respect [10]:

---

[8]   Some shares may have no voting rights while others may lead to multiple votes.
[9]   According to the BCCI-directive (1993) control means "the relationship between a parent enterprise and a subsidiary (as defined in Article 1 of directive 83/349/EEC - OJEC) or a similar relationship between any natural or legal person and an enterprise.
[10]   See e.g. definition of a group in Moret & Limperg (1985), CEA (1993) and Burgert, Timmermans and Joosten (1990).

- the Belgian consolidation legislation[11] states that a majority in the capital is not a correct measure of control, because some shares may have no voting rights while others may lead to multiple votes; according to the Belgian legislator it is not the formal legal position but the economic reality that is the key indicator; therefore "effective control" is the only relevant measure and a distinction has to be made between "formal legal" control and "factual" control:
  * legal power of control exists if a company possesses the majority of the voting rights (parent /subsidiary) or has a decisive influence on the nomination (or the dismissal?) of (the majority) of directors or on the orientation of strategy and management;
  * there is no legal basis for control but a "factual" presumption if the enterprise represented the majority of the votes in the two previous shareholders' meetings;
- according to Börner (1993), the amount of 20% of the voting rights in the BCCI-directive is an incorrect indicator, because what counts is the real economic influence.
- in the U.K.[12], a "dependent" company is defined as a company in which the parent (insurance company) has at least one third of the voting rights.

Most relevant definitions however refer to both criteria:

- the definitions of qualifying holdings and participations, set out in paragraph 1.2.1., are mostly based on both criteria (ownership or voting rights, c.q. effective control or influence);
- also the consolidation methods for credit institutions make the distinction between majority ownership, effective control and participations that are neither (see e.g. OJEC 83/350/EC).

1.2.4. ECONOMIC VERSUS LEGAL INTEGRATION

The great diversity in the degree of integration, from a financial as well as from a marketing, a functional and/or a legal perspective, leads to a scattered landscape of financial conglomerates.

Moreover it is clear that a financial participation must not necessarily lead to an operational integration. As can be proved by some interesting definitions of financial conglomerates, a financial conglomerate has not to be restricted to groups in the strict legal sense of the word[13]. Also marketing arrangements and joint ventures can lead to a combined offering of financial products, investments, and/or

---

[11] KB 06.03.1990 (BS 27.03.1990), changed by KB 30.12.1991 (BS 31.12.1991) and KB 03.12.1993 (BS 23.12.1993).
[12] CEA (1993).
[13] See e.g. - EC-definition EC-DG XV - 110/85 and the definition of Koguchi (1993).

insurance products[14].

Thorough analysis learns that quite a lot of models can be used (at least in theory) to set up a financial conglomerate[15] :

- the completely integrated financial conglomerate, where the different business activities are integrated into one legal entity; this resembles the German universal banking principle (it is however not possible to include also insurance activities within the universal bank);
- the integrated financial conglomerate which establishes chinese walls to separate part of the activities in order to prevent conflicts of interest;
- an integrated legal system but with an operational separation in order to protect certain types of functions (e.g. an integrated group with collateralized deposits or savings);
- a bank parent with non-bank subsidiaries: the parent company is the bank and the non-bank activities are conducted in one or more seperately incorporated subsidiaries; this construction resembles some British cases;
- an insurance parent with financial subsidiaries; some insurers diversifying into assurfinance use this model (e.g. in The Netherlands);
- participations (majority, minority) of banks in insurance companies or vice versa;
- a holding company which owns the banking and non-banking subsidiaries and which integrates an important number of functions and activities (e.g. referrals, cross-selling, mixed products, intra-group financing, etc.); this formula resembles the US-model of bank holding companies; according to the Dutch central bank (1992), such a holding is called a mixed holding company; subsidiaries which are combinations of credit and insurance activities are called "bancassurance" by Moret Ernst & Young (1993);
- a holding company which owns the banking and non-banking subsidiaries but without an (important) operational integration; here the group is more an investment holding than a financial conglomerate; the Belgian holdings have been relying on this model for quite a long time;
- joint venture formulas, whereby the different sectoral corporations jointly set up a new establishment for integrated services, innovative mixed products or

---

[14]   According to recent scientifical research the hypothesis is defended that full ownership is preferable if a diversifying firm is looking for specificity; on the contrary collaboration formulas are more economical if resource constraints are the reason for the diversification (see Ingham, H. & Thompson, S. - 1994).
Not legal prescriptions but economic optimisation should decide what structure is best suited to set up a financial conglomerate (see European Insurance Market (1994).

[15]   Herring & Santomero (1990) limited their analysis to 5 types. They ignored the insurance holding formula as well as all forms of participations, joint ventures and collaboration.
Koguchi (1993) ignored the formation of financial conglomerates in which insurers take the lead.

cross-selling;
- sales and marketing agreements without ownership linkages for (exclusive or non-exclusive) cross-selling etc.

For the sake of simplicity, we would suggest to make a distinction based on the degree of both the legal and operational integration:

- financial conglomerates in the strict sense: the members of the group are linked through qualifying holdings and have a common strategy and mutual responsibilities;
- financial conglomerates in the broadest sense: the partners are not linked through qualifying holdings (less than 20%) but they have a marketing joint venture with common trade names or distribution agreements so that the entrepreneurial risks are combined in an indirect manner; necessary conditions in this respect are the "lasting" character of the cooperation and the interaction between the business activities involved;
- financial conglomerates without any economic integration: included here are financial conglomerates (corporations with at least a qualifying holding-structure) whose members have no common strategy or which corporations have no operational integration at all;

it is questionable whether this last category can be considered as a financial conglomerate; it might be classified as an "investment holding" or a "participation company" (see Moret & Limperg - 1985).

1.3. DEFINING FINANCIAL INSTITUTIONS AND FINANCIAL ACTIVITIES

Most basic literature on financial institutions makes a distinction between the financial markets (money market, capital market -primary market, secondary market-), the financial instruments (products, activities) and the financial institutions. The whole is then defined as the financial system.
For this analysis it is important to look more thoroughly at the definition of financial institutions. Financial institutions can be defined as enterprises whose assets and liabilities consist almost exclusively of financial instruments (direct and/or indirect financial assets).
The term financial institutions covers a wide variety of organisations. The most relevant categories in this respect are[16] :

- financial intermediaries whose basic characteristic is that they act as intermediary between economic agents with financial surpluses (supply of funds) and

[16]   See e.g. Van den Berghe (1983) & Wytzes (1978).

those with financial shortages (demand of funds);
according to the type of titles they issue (liabilities), a distinction can be made between monetary institutions and non-monetary institutions :

* the monetary institutions who issue monetary instruments; these can be defined as financial instruments that are accepted for their nominal value as "payment instruments"; examples in this respect are banks and savings banks;

* non-monetary financial intermediaries, who do not issue monetary instruments but who act as financial intermediaries; examples in this respect are mortgage banks;

- institutional investors: whose primary function is not to act as a financial intermediary, but their primary function induces an important financial function; this means that through their core business they collect money which they have to invest; consequently their asset activities (investments) are always subordinate to their commitments towards their clients (liabilities); most of the literature limits the "institutional investors" - category to the life insurance companies and pension funds (see e.g. Wytzes - 1978); we have showed that also non-life insurance companies act as financial institutions (Van den Berghe - 1981): the only relevant distinction that has to be made in this respect is whether the financial function is induced by the insurance technique (investment of the technical reserves) or whether the financial function is also a consequence of the fact that insurers attract saving money (saving premium, capitalisation products, unit linked products, etc.).

The EC-directives do not give a clear definition of a financial institution; they only enumerate what types of enterprises can be considered as financial institutions[17]:

- a bank,
- a savings bank,
- an institution specialising in the provision of short, medium or long term debt, (these three are considered to be credit institutions)
- an insurance company,
- a building society,
- an investment company
- and equivalent institutions.

The national definitions of what enterprises form the "financial institution - sector" will differ according to historical situations and differences (see e.g. the definition of the Central Bank of Ireland (1992) and the application to the Netherlands (Scholtens - 1993)).
Interesting in this respect is the definition given by the Bank of England (1987)

---

[17] Directive on the liberalisation of capital movements, OJEC 86/566/EC.

which states that a financial institution or a group of financial institutions must have financial activities (as listed above) as its main business; in this respect main business is defined in relation to the balance sheet total: at least 50% of its balance sheet total must be related to financial activities.

Some definitions refer to the specific activities covered by the institutions under consideration. Credit institutions are then defined as follows :

> "...whose business broadly is to receive deposits or other repayable funds from the public and, on the other hand, to grant credits for its own account"[18].

Consequently investment firms (or securities business), investment funds (UCITS or undertakings for collective investment in transferable securities) and insurance companies do not fall within the scope of credit institutions. For a more detailed list of activities carried out by credit institutions see e.g. OJEC 77/780/EC.

1.4. WHAT DISTINGUISHES A FINANCIAL CONGLOMERATE FROM A FINANCIAL INSTITUTION?

The most often used distinction between financial institutions and financial conglomerates, especially in documents, published by the European Commission and the national supervisory authorities - is that the former are supervised by one specific supervisory authority, while the latter contains institutions that are subjected to different types of supervision (see e.g. CEA (1993), Pearson (1991), Clarotti (1992), Brittan (1991)).

Besides this "regulatory" distinction between a financial institution and a financial conglomerate, one can also refer to the "economic" definition of a "concern". In the general literature on business strategy, the distinction is made between the strategy of a "strategic business unit or SBU" and the "corporate" strategy. The latter refers to the complete set of activities, SBU's and enterprises forming the larger entity of the "corporation" or "concern". A SBU is often defined as the part of the corporation (either with or without a specific legal status) that operates within one specific economic sector[19]. Consequently a concern is defined as a group of companies or SBU's which operate in different economic sectors. This general economic approach has also been used to define financial conglomerates. The following different views exist as to what sectors compose a financial conglomerate:

---

[18] First council directive on the coordination of credit institutions, OJEC 77/780/EC; see also Pearson (1991).

[19] See e.g. S.W. Douma, (1990).

- at least one bank and one insurance undertaking (see FEE (1994), Pearson (1991), Protocol DNB & VK (1990), Protocol DNB & VK (1994));
- at least two of the three potential sectors, namely credit institutions, investment institutions or securities business and insurance companies (see Börner (1993) and CEA (1993)); reference is also made to "some other financial services" (see IOSCO (1992)).

If a financial conglomerate only combines credit institutions and investment firms the problems involved are different from the case that also insurance companies are included (see Clarotti (1992)).

1.5.   COMPLEMENTARITY BETWEEN THE ACTIVITIES AND INSTITUTIONS INVOLVED

One of the specific features of a financial conglomerate is that it combines activities with a certain degree of complementarity. The definition given by the European Commission is certainly instructive in this respect :

> "different types of complementary financial services are combined within one group; the financial activities must form the most important part of the business of this group; if otherwise, the group is not seen as a financial conglomerate but merely as a "mixed" conglomerate"[20].

Such a mixed conglomerate may not be confused with a mixed financial conglomerate. In fact, from a regulatory perspective the distinction is often made between:

- homogeneous financial institutions: falling within the scope of one economic sector and one supervisory system; here consolidation of supervision will eventually be demanded;
- groups with a predominantly financial character, which also include one or more insurance companies;
- groups with a predominantly insurance character, which also include one or more banking institutions;
- groups with a considerable banking and insurance business, referred to as mixed financial conglomerates.[21]

Different sources agree that only conglomerates that contain a considerable amount of financial and insurance services should be considered as financial conglomerates (see e.g. Clarotti (1992), Koguchi (1993), Pearson (1991), Protocol DNB & VK (1990) and IOSCO (1992)).
Others however find that also "mixed" conglomerates should be included. Scholtens

---

[20]   P. Clarotti, (1992).
[21]   See e.g. CDV (1992-93) and Protocol DNB & VK (1990).

(1993) makes the distinction between financial conglomerates with mainly financial activities and financial conglomerates with significant industrial and trade activities.

It is not only important to see whether the regulation of financial conglomerates should make a distinction between the mixed conglomerates and the pure financial conglomerates, but it is also necessary to make a distinction between the mixed financial conglomerates and the rather marginally diversified financial and insurance groups. This is the case in the Netherlands, where through the Protocol between the Dutch Central Bank and the Insurance Supervisor, the diversified financial groups are controlled by the first supervisor, while the latter controls the diversified insurance groups; only the mixed financial conglomerates are under the combined supervision of both institutions.

This definition seems more straigthforward than it really is. The question in fact is until what degree a diversification into a complementary activity is considered as being marginal and from what moment on a financial conglomerate becomes a mixed financial conglomerate. What statistical criteria should be used to make this distinction?

A recent research (Joosten (1994)) limited the analysis of financial conglomerates to those groups who had at least 10% of their turnover in the different sectors involved.

The FEE (1994) suggested that abbreviated disclosures should be allowed for financial conglomerates with minor relationships in diversified activities. Minor relationships are defined as follows:

where two out of three of the following criteria are met (during the current and two previous years):

- balance sheet total is less than 10% of the group total,
- net turnover[22] is less than 10% of the group total,
- average number of employees is less than 10% of the group total.

In our practical research we investigated the relative importance of the different activities involved. This is a difficult task since there is no obligation for consolidated accounts. Moreover, the different activities involved can not be compared that easily. Nevertheless we tried to test these aspects for some financial conglomerates.

To measure the relative weight of the banking and insurance activities we used the following indicators:

---

[22] As defined in the Banking Accounting Directive and Insurance Accounting Directive.

- balance sheet total
- total turnover[23].

1.6.   A FINANCIAL CONGLOMERATE IS NOT REALLY A CONGLOMERATE IN THE ECONOMIC SENSE OF THE WORD

The term "financial conglomerate" creates potential misunderstanding and misinterpretation since it's meaning is quite different from the notion of "industrial conglomerates". Here again the pure translation of industrial principles to the financial business proves to be (partly) incorrect.

Industrial conglomerates, which were established decennia ago, all had the main characteristic of combining completely different activities within one holding structure. The management literature (see e.g. P. Kotler (1994)) used this "diversification" to make the distinction between :

- "concentric" diversification: which is a diversification into related products or services so that parallel technology and marketing can be used;
- "horizontal" diversification: is a diversification into complementary products so that parallel technology but a different marketing approach has to be used;
- "conglomerate diversification": is a diversification into completely different activities with a complety different technology and oriented towards different markets.

Financial conglomerates are "characterised by an additional important element that is often lacking in their industrial or commercial counterparts, and that is a high degree of complementarity between the services provided by the different parts of the organisation"[24].
The aim of a financial conglomerate is mainly to exploit the synergies which exist between banking, insurance and investment. Consequently it is not a "conglomerate diversification" and the basic literature on industrial conglomerates is better to be ignored because it could be more than misleading. This is certainly true for the literature on the failures of industrial conglomerates.

> "The fact that a number of the industrial conglomerates ....fell apart, might suggest that a similar fate awaits some financial groups. It is doubtful, however, whether previous experience is altogether relevant in this con-

---

[23]   Defined as follows:
    - for banks: the total of interest income and other revenues (including fee income, commissions, etc.);
    - for insurance companies: the (direct) insurance premiums and the financial revenues and other income (for more details see chapter 3).

[24]   Maycock, J. (1986), see also Gardener, E.P.M. (1987).

text. Many of the industrial conglomerates were the outcome of attempts to bring under the same organisational umbrella elements that by their nature were often quite disparate, acquisitions were often made only in order to "strip assets". They lacked industrial logic. For the most part, by contrast, the services provided by a financial conglomerate have a common relationship that carries with it a degree of cohesion. In other words, all parts of a financial conglomerate are ultimately dealing in the same commodity."[25]

Since the term "financial conglomerate" is already used in so many circles we will stick to this term but with the clear warning that it does not relate to the concept of an industrial conglomerate.

[25]   Maycock, J. (1986).

Appendix I.A.

Defining financial conglomerates: Relevant definitions

The definitions in this appendix are arranged in chronological order.

A.1. DEFINING A GROUP

A group can be defined as a combination of companies and legal entities that form an economic unity under coordinated control and in which the leading corporation has decisive power and control over the other group members (Moret & Limperg - 1994); see also CEA (1993).

The Dutch Civil Code (1990) on the contrary concentrates the definition of a group company on the following criteria:

- the corporations form an economic entity and operate under joint management;
- a group relation is based on a majority participation; but also a minority share can lead to a "group" company as far as this share is strenghtened with special rights or special arrangements.

A group company is defined in Bank of England (1992) as a company that is consolidated (for reporting purposes) with the other institution involved or that would be consolidated if it were not supervised by another (UK) supervisory authority.

Börner (1993) gives the following definition of a group:
"Überdacht werden sollte allerdings die in Artikel 1 vorgesehene Definition der "GRUPPE". Nach Artikel 1 a) ist als Schwellenwert für die Zugehörigkeit zu einer Gruppe das direkte oder indirekte Halten von mindestens 20% der Stimmrechte oder des Kapitals an einem anderen Unternehmen gewählt worden. Ich halte diesen Schwellenwert für zu niedrig. Abgestellt werden sollte hier vielmehr auf die tatsächlichen unternehmerischen Einflussmöglichkeiten (vergleiche Artikel 1 der siebten Richtlinie über den konsolidierten Abschluss)."

A.2. **DEFINING A DAUGHTER COMPANY OR SUBSIDIARY**

A branch (of a credit institution) is defined by the EC (in OJEC 77/780/EC) as follows:
"a place of business which forms a legally dependent part of a credit institution and which carries out directly all or some of the transactions inherent in the business of a credit institution; any number of places of business set up in the same member state by a credit institution with its head office situated in another member state shall be regarded as a single branch."

If a corporation owns (directly and indirectly - through other subsidiaries or group companies) more than 50% of another company, the latter can be seen as a subsidiary or a daughter-company of the first one (mother-company) (Moret & Limperg -1994).

In the Belgian consolidation regulations[26] a subsidiary is defined in a broader way:

- majority of shares
- majority of votes
- nomination of the majority of the directors
- factual power of control.

A.3. **DEFINING A PARTICIPATION**

A participation is supposed to exist (legally) from the moment a corporation owns at least 20% of another enterprise.
According to a Dutch source (Moret & Limperg -1994), this legal supposition is ignored if the economic reality gives opposing evidence; this means that a holding of more than 20% is not considered as a participation from the moment that this holding has no "permanent" character or if there is no link between the activities of the two corporations.

A.4. **DEFINING AN ASSOCIATED OR RELATED ENTERPRISE**

In the Belgian consolidation legislation[27] a holding has a "significant influence" on the management of an "associated or related enterprise if the former owns at least 20% of the latter.

---

[26]   KB 06.03.1990 (BS 27.03.1990), changed by KB 30.12.1991 (BS 31.12.1991) and KB 03.12.1993 (BS 23.12.1993).
[27]   See footnote 26.

For participations in an "associated" enterprise no consolidation will be obliged, but equity accounting is possible[28].

A.5. DEFINING A FINANCIAL CONGLOMERATE

In her first working paper, the European Commission gave the following definition[29]:
"Financial Conglomerate is a body made up of one company or several companies which offer to the public (private individuals as well as commercial or industrial customers) a range of services either entirely financial or financial and non-financial together. The financial products sold in this way are of different kinds, or represent activities supervised by more than one authority, or both. When they are supplied by a group of several companies those companies are linked to one another by majority holdings or effective control so that joint marketing and mutual responsibilities go together (Financial Conglomerate in the strict sense). Where this is not the case, but where financial products are nevertheless marketed jointly (same trade mark; agency arrangements, etc.) one can speak of a Financial Conglomerate in a wider sense if the risks assumed by one component of the conglomerate indirectly involve the others. The range of conglomerate services as a whole displays complementary products, techniques, or the interests of the component companies are complementary; this range can be homogeneous (all services concern the credit industries) or mixed (the services stem from various financial sectors) or heterogeneous (the range includes non-financial services or goods). The Financial Conglomerate idea can be disregarded where the financial activity is only marginal inside a wider concern."

The working group of insurance supervisors of the European Union gives the following definition (1992):
"A *financial conglomerate* is understood to be a clearly defined economic group comprising financial institutions, which are subject to supervision in terms of Community law, from at least two of the following categories - credit institutions, insurance companies or investment institutions - which licensed institutions collectively constitute a substantial interest in the group."

General conglomerate:
There is an economic unit under uniform management, but financial institutions do not account for a predominant share.

A *separate financial group* does not comprise an economic unit but a complex of closely affiliated financial institution.

---

[28]   This is the case when the enterprises' activities are not related one to another.
[29]   E.C.- D.G.XV - 110/85.

In general, the countries support the tripartite division into financial conglomerates, general conglomerates and separate financial groups.

The definition given by IOSCO (1992) is the following:
"the term "financial conglomerate" is used to refer to any group of companies under common ownership where financial activities -whether securities business, banking, insurance and some other financial services- are undertaken on a significant scale by one or more companies in the group".

Other definitions given by IOSCO [Report on financial conglomerates; working group of insurance supervisiors (1992)] are:

Para-financial conglomerates:
General conglomerates whose financial activities exert such influence that de facto it is possible to consider them as financial conglomerates.

Quasi-financial conglomerates:
Any conglomerate comprising at least one financial institution under supervision.

Koguchi (1993) gives the following definition:
"At present, there is no generally-agreed or standard definition of a financial conglomerate. In this note, the term is used as to refer to an equity-related corporate group made up of several companies which offers a range of services either entirely financial or predominantly of a financial nature ....
An alternative and broader concept of financial conglomerate would regard it as an entity which offers to the public a range of services either entirely financial or financial and non-financial together. The financial products sold in this way must be of different kinds, or represent activities supervised by more than one authority, or both. When they are supplied by a group made up by several companies, those companies are linked through majority holdings or effective control so that joint marketing and mutual responsibilities go together. Where this is not the case the concept of financial conglomeration can still be applied whenever financial products are marketed jointly if the risks assumed by a component of the conglomerate indirectly involve the others."

The definition given by CEA (1993) for Spain is the following:
Group of financial undertakings: groups formed by undertakings belonging to the same financial sector or different financial sectors.

The definition given by DNB & VK (1994) is the following:
A *financial conglomerate* with at least one credit institution and at least one insurance company established in The Netherlands. Banking and insurance activities must be a considerable part of the activities according to the Dutch Central

Bank (DNB) and the Dutch Chamber of Insurance (VK). The banking and insurance activities together, must be at least 50% of the total consolidated balance sheet.

Conglomerate: a group in which the corporations form an economic entity and are organisationally connected.

2. **Defining financial conglomerates**

Discussion

2.1. DISCUSSION BY DR. A. J. VERMAAT[1]

2.1.1. ONE OR MORE DEFINITIONS ?

As is commonly accepted in academic literature on the methodology of a discipline, it is seldom satisfactory to look for a single complementary and satisfactory definition of a given concept. It is often more effective to work with a number of mutually differentiated definitive concepts, that is, concepts which vary in terms of the specific use of the concept in relation to the problem definition or context.

This also applies to the concept of a financial conglomerate. It might as well be the case that an analysis for the purpose of supervision may require a different typology than an analysis of conglomerate formation in general (theory of the external organisation/ theory of industrial relations), or an analysis of the financial sector in relation to monetary policy. Naturally there is no objection to the various approaches using the same set of definitions. It must, however, be possible to do so. In other words, effectiveness must have priority over efficiency!

In some instances a more general concept may be used in addition to a number of different groups with differentiated sub-definitions in order to describe sub-types within the general group. An example is the variety used for money supply definitions.

2.1.2. GENERAL THEORY OF CONGLOMERATES

Paragraph 1.6. deals with the question whether a financial conglomerate is a conglomerate or not - this on the basis of the general theory of industrial relations. Personally I have less difficulty with the use of the term "conglomerate" to describe financial conglomerates. Even if the average characteristics of an industrial conglomerate differs from those of a financial conglomerate and even if the explanatory factors behind the formation of such industrial conglomerates are different to those of financial conglomerates, there is no objection to the use of the

---

[1] President of the Verzekeringskamer, the Netherlands.

term "conglomerate" in two mutually divergent applications. After all, the difference in adjective may already point to the mutual distinction. Furthermore, the word "industrial" has a far wider application in terms of scope - and consequently in terms of sub-sectors - than the term "financial". Nevertheless, there is a clear anology in relation to both terms. The crucial characteristic which is signified by the term "conglomerate" is that incongruous components are grouped together - at least when viewed from a particular perspective! This coincides with the general meaning of the etymological root "conglomeratum" (Latin) or "conglomérat" (French). The basic meaning of these words is: clustered together, piled up, compressed together or stuck together.

Chapter 1 places much emphasis on the fact that industrial conglomerates by definition *must* have a very "heterogeneous" character. This does not seem to me to be correct, neither theoretically, nor empirically[2]. Can it be said, for instance, that Philips', Unilever's or Shell's internal formation is so strongly heterogeneous, or that they may not be referred to as industrial conglomerates?

Furthermore the designation of "incongruity" by the term "conglomerate" is always accompanied by the notion that the various components have been grouped into a single "unit". This is incidentally also included in the geological meaning of the term "conglomerate ", that is, various sorts of rock fused together by a physical process as if by a natural cement!

In the case of financial conglomerates there is, in my view, sufficient evidence of, on the one hand, a certain form of differentiation (in other words, various sub-sectors of the financial sector) and, on the other hand, the formation of a "unit". That the financial sector is by its very nature smaller in scope and relatively less heterogeneous than the industrial sector gives rise to a difference in degree, but not to a fundamental dissimilarity.

With a view to a good, and therefore clear typology, another additional (new) term is perhaps needed, namely a concept which can logically include both the sub-concepts of a financial conglomerate and an industrial conglomerate . This may be found in another English term: "conglomeration". In my view, this is not strictly necessary.

2.1.3. THE TERM "FINANCIAL CONGLOMERATE" IN THE CONTEXT OF SUPERVISION

As a result from a literature study I could not find the precise meaning which was originally given to the term " financial conglomerate" (and when or by whom?). I

---

[2]   Note of the editor: Although this is the case in most of the literature.

do know this term was used in the eighties in relation to issues regarding to supervision. A certain definition has become common amongst supervisors (cf. paragraph 1.1.). For instance (see also appendix 2.A.):

> "A financial conglomerate is understood to be a clearly defined economic group comprising financial institutions, which are subject to supervision in terms of Community law, from at least two of the following categories - credit institutions, insurance companies or investment institutions - which licensed institutions collectively constitute a substantial interest in the group."

This definition has been taken from the report of the working group set up by the Conference of Insurance Supervisors of the European Community with regard to Financial Conglomerates, 1992 (page 5).

This report was also based on earlier work for the Conference carried out by the Insurance Supervisory Board in 1990 and linked to a preparatory study by the Insurance Supervisory Board together with the Dutch Central Bank which provided a common protocol for co-ordinated supervision of insurance companies and credit institutions respectively in the context of a group which could be characterised as a financial conglomerate. Financial conglomerates did exist in the Netherlands for several years (despite the so-called "structure policy" which was intended to avert the formation of such financial conglomerates). The Insurance Supervisory Board made a creative contribution, amongst others, to the terminology (later) used in the Protocol, of which the sub-typology is of particular importance, that is, the tripartite subdivision into a) primarily banking financial conglomerates b) primarily insurance financial conglomerates, and c) (genuine) mixed financial conglomerates. For pragmatic reasons the criterion used for the subdivision in this regard is the 80/20 percentage boundary based on a total legally required solvency margin.

In addition to the concept of a financial conglomerate (whereby at least 50% of the balance sheet total - or possibly of another total indicator - originates from financial institutions within the concern) there are also the complementary concepts: a not primarily financial conglomerate (that is a conglomerate which consists of a substantial, but not a majority (in other words, less than 50%), share of financial subsidiaries within the concern or, alternatively, a general conglomerate (with a non-substantial portion of licensed financial subsidiaries).

2.1.4. AN ATTEMPT TO A SIMPLE TYPOLOGY

Chapter 1 contains a lot of information on the various facets of the discussion with regard to the characterisation on demarcation of financial conglomerates, but gives no clear proof of an operationally applicable typology. The following is a contribution to such a general typology (see scheme).

At a basic level, what is at issue, is the legally defined operating unit: the single firm or company.

The *first* subdivision includes companies which are not dependent on others (in other words, "solo firms") and those companies which are dependent (in other words, "member firms" or "induced firms").

The *second* subdivision includes those companies which form part of a loose "group" (a "network" group can possibly be used to describe these) and companies which are part of an economic group which is genuinely internally integrated (on the basis of, firstly, directive power held by a central holding company within the group and/or, secondly, the exceeding of minimum participation percentages of 25% to 33%). The term "economic group" should be reserved for such companies.

The *third* subdivision includes more or less heterogeneous economic groups (in other words, the "conglomerates") and the more or less homogeneous economic groups (that is, the "concerns").

The *fourth* subdivision includes financial and non-financial conglomerates (with the possibility of further subdividing the latter into general and mixed conglomerates).

Finally, as the *fifth* subdivision, a distinction can be made in: a) mixed financial conglomerates and b) specialised financial conglomerates (that is, those in which a sub-type of financial company dominates). This latter group includes, for instance, primarily banking (credit/securities) financial conglomerates, insurance financial conglomerates and investment financial conglomerates. If necessary, a distinction can also be made, as far as terminology is concerned, in financial companies under supervision ("financial institutions") and financial companies which are not under supervision ("other financial firms").

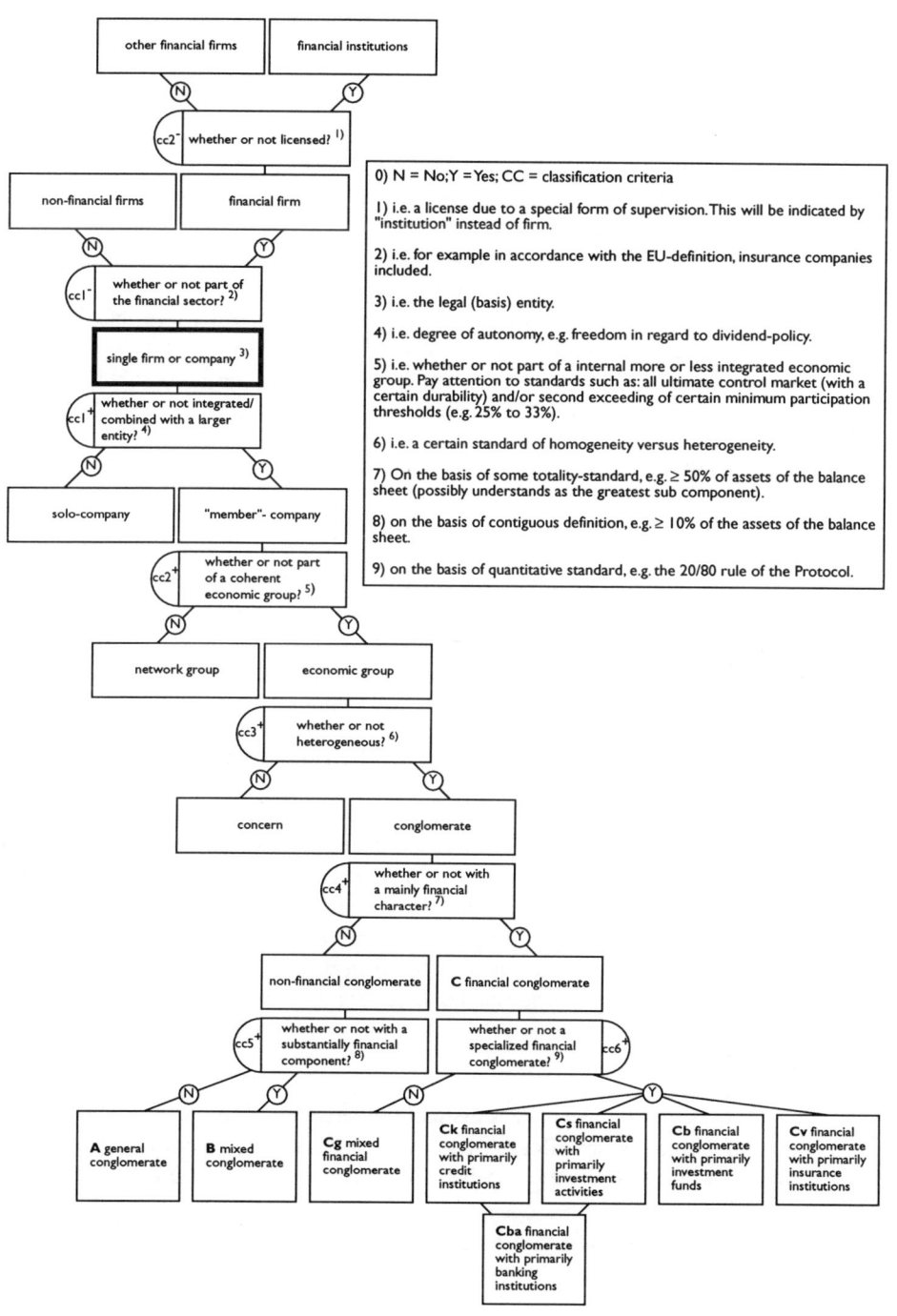

0) N = No; Y = Yes; CC = classification criteria

1) i.e. a license due to a special form of supervision. This will be indicated by "institution" instead of firm.

2) i.e. for example in accordance with the EU-definition, insurance companies included.

3) i.e. the legal (basis) entity.

4) i.e. degree of autonomy, e.g. freedom in regard to dividend-policy.

5) i.e. whether or not part of a internal more or less integrated economic group. Pay attention to standards such as: all ultimate control market (with a certain durability) and/or second exceeding of certain minimum participation thresholds (e.g. 25% to 33%).

6) i.e. a certain standard of homogeneity versus heterogeneity.

7) On the basis of some totality-standard, e.g. ≥ 50% of assets of the balance sheet (possibly understands as the greatest sub component).

8) on the basis of contiguous definition, e.g. ≥ 10% of the assets of the balance sheet.

9) on the basis of quantitative standard, e.g. the 20/80 rule of the Protocol.

2.2. **DISCUSSION BY DRS. J.H. HOLSBOER**[3]

2.2.1. DEFINITION:

I prefer the term Group rather than Conglomerate, which has a somewhat negative connotation. In the comprehensive Van Dale dictionary a conglomerate is described as an accidental coagulation of unequal parts.

I know at least one financial group which has certainly not been accidentally founded, but as a consequence of a well considered strategic decision; which was not coagulated, but merged out of fully equal parts!

Chapter 1 mentioned that only the Spanish legislation provides a formal definition of a financial conglomerate.[4] However also the Dutch Protocol, which deserves special attention and interest in this context, contains a very workable and pragmatic definition for Financial Conglomerates.

2.2.2. LEVEL PLAYING FIELD

Maintaining a level playing field should be an important precondition for any form of supervision on financial conglomerates. An (extra) argument for this can be found in the more or less arbitrary definition of a financial conglomerate. This should be solved pragmatically. But without a level playing field there will be arbitrary changes in competitive relations.

We should strive for a form of supervision (also for 'cross-border bancassurance') which has the advantages of 'solo-plus', while maintaining a level playing field.

2.2.3. PARTICIPATION VERSUS INVESTMENT AND THE 'DROIT DE SUITE'

Several definitions of the various relationships between companies which may or may not be part of a group are discussed in the workshop papers. An important element is the definition threshold for a 'participation' in another enterprise, in which case the 'droit de suite' applies, the right of access for a supervisor to any relevant information. In the 'post BCCI-directive' and in a draft version of a possible EC-directive on the supervision of insurance operations in an insurance group a participation is defined as the direct or indirect ownership of 20% or more of the voting rights or capital of an undertaking. I have serious objections to this threshold definition:

- first, we should make a clear distinction between situations where the participating company has effective control over or voting power in the 'subsidiary' undertaking and situations where no such control or voting power can be

---

[3]   Member of the Executive Board of ING, the Netherlands.
[4]   Note of the editor: This was not a general statement but related to the conclusions of the CEA-analysis.

exercised;

- in addition, even where 20% of the votes are held I cannot see how a 'droit de suite' could be made effective (and legally enforced, for instance outside the EC);
- ownership of non-voting stock should never have consequences for supervision.

In conclusion we strongly favour a pragmatic and workable regulation!

2.3.   DISCUSSION BY DR. K.W. KNAUTH [5]

2.3.2. WHAT ARE THE ESSENTIAL ELEMENTS THAT CONSTITUTE A FINANCIAL CONGLOMERATE?

The analysis presented in chapter 1 shows that the term "financial conglomerate" gives rise to misinterpretations because in economics this term is associated with industrial conglomerates. In Germany it has so far been more or less unknown. The word "conglomerate" has a rather negative connotation. It describes an unorganized structure of different things which really do not belong together. Therefore, many voices were raised among German insurers pointing out the wrong choice of the word. It would be more correct to use the term "mixed group" because it is of nothing else that we are talking.
However, it is also wrong to use the term "mixed financial services group".
The supervisory authorities never raised the question whether all companies in a financial conglomerate are in fact financial institutions. This gave rise to the impression that the supervisory considerations concern companies whose objects are largely identical.

In the discussion on financial conglomerates it is - at least from the German point of view - unjustified to extend this assumption to insurance companies. There is no such thing as a homogeneous insurance business which might be compared to the business of, for instance, a universal bank. The insurance business, as a whole, is carried on by different insurance companies (principle of specialization).

The centre and origin of the insurance business is the risks business. With regard to this business, the policyholder transfers the economic risks of a possible event of loss to the insurance company which, in turn, balances the risks it has accepted by using its portfolio on a collective basis. With one insured the possible loss occurs, with another it does not. According to the German point of view, it would be bold to describe this by the term "financial service".

---

[5]   Gesamtverband der Deutschen Versicherungswirtschaft e.V., Germany.

However, especially in life assurance the risks business is linked to the savings business. In that case, the policyholder does not only pay a premium for the covering of the risk, but also a certain amount for savings purposes, which is invested by the insurance company in an interest-bearing form. The savings operation is similar to the deposit business of the banks, however, the insurer's operation includes two aspects which are generally missing in the case of a bank. First, the savings operation is safeguarded by insurance. Secondly, unlike the saver of a bank, the insured is not able to demand his savings deposit back at any time, but in most cases only after ten or twenty years. Therefore, a liquidity crisis in the form of a "bank run", which is always feared by banks, is not possible even for those types of insurance which are linked to a savings operation. That is why, in this case as well, I hesitate to describe at least long-term life assurance by the term "financial service" in the banking sense.

The advocates of the term "financial institute" used for banks, investments firms and insurance companies will argue that what is relevant in this respect is the investments made in the same way by banks and insurance companies.
This, however, is already contradicted by the Second Banking Directive and the Third Insurance Directives which have opened the EC Single Market for banks and insurance companies. In these directives, the investments made by insurance companies are regulated by detailed spreading and diversification rules. Such rules are lacking in the case of banks, the only exception are the rules on large exposures which have just been adopted.

The choice of the term "financial institution" is probably also largely due to the fact that the discussion on financial conglomerates has been started by representatives of international banking supervision. However, the Basle Committee on Banking Supervision comprises not only European, but also, for instance, American and Japanese banking supervisors. In considering the problem, it were above all US American ideas which gained importance. However, their concept of the nature of the investments made by an insurance company is basically different from the concepts of most European insurers:

- According to the American concept, an insurance company, similar to a credit institution, is a financial institution. The investment business is the main business of an insurance company, and the insurance business only serves to procure the funds for this main business which pursues the primary aim of maximizing yield.
- According to the European concept, the investments made by insurance companies serve the insurance business. Investment is a consequence of the prepayment of the insurance premium and the carrying on of the savings business.

The above statements lead to the conclusion that it would not be correct to describe insurance companies in Europe by the term "financial institutions". Moreover, their activity may not be equated with that of banks or investments firms. It would be even better to use the term "mixed group" to make clear the different nature of the products offered by the individual companies. For that reason, I also disagree with the conclusion of the analysis carried out by the Erasmus Finance & Insurance Centre, i.e. that in the end all companies in a financial conglomerate deal with the same product.

2.3.2. DEFINING A GROUP OF ENTERPRISES

The Erasmus Finance & Insurance Centre has also very carefully pointed out the different possibilities on the question how large a holding in a company must be to assume the existence of a group.

However, precise criteria are necessary with regard to the classification of companies. This is particularly true in consideration of the supervisory consequences which the classification under a group should have. It should not be forgotten that the discussion on financial conglomerates has been caused by the fear of the banking supervisors that economic difficulties experienced by a company in a group might be transferred to other companies in the same group or, at least, causes an obligation to provide financial assistance.

According to the ideas of the international supervisory authorities which have so far become known, these risks in a group are to be reduced by a form of consolidation the details of which have not yet been decided on. Therefore, it is necessary to choose as a criterion for the definition the actual possibility of the management to influence another company. However, this exists only in the case of a majority holding or if a company is able to exert a dominating influence on another company. For that reason, I advocate not going a special way but recognizing the definition of the group contained in Art. 1 of the Seventh Directive on Consolidated Accounts (83/349/EEC of 13 June 1983) - which is established and has been tried and tested - as a prerequisite for the existence of a group also in this case.

2.4.   DISCUSSION BY P. PEARSON[6]

2.4.1. SEEKING A LEGAL DEFINITION OF A FINANCIAL CONGLOMERATE

Until now, no legal definition of a financial conglomerate has been developed. A number of questions arise when a legal definition is sought for *supervisory* purposes, which is the main objective of the European Commission's work. The supervisory objectives may require at a certain point in time translation into legal terms. The definition of a financial conglomerate in discussions at the level of the

---

[6]   DG XV, European Commission.

EU will therefore of necessity always be based on legal considerations, rather than economical, tax, or otherwise. As referred to in chapter 1, at present only Spain has a definition of a financial conglomerate in its national supervisory law.

One of the difficulties related to the elaboration of a definition of a financial conglomerate is the fact that any definition is inextricably linked with the purpose it serves. Clarity on that purpose has to be achieved first. The definition of the financial conglomerate must describe the 'group'[7] of undertakings to which certain supervisory rules should be applied. There exist several areas of possible rule-making for which the scope must be defined (intra-group cross-holdings, large exposures etc.).

The most important of these areas in the Commission's view is the prevention of double gearing. It is therefore suggested to confine the definition of a "financial conglomerate" to a 'group' of undertakings to which rules on the prevention (or detection) of double gearing should be applied. At the same time, this restriction means that for each of any other areas of possible legislative action the scope must be defined separately.

The approach preferred by the Commission is therefore to define for each rule its relevant scope rather than seeking to find an abstract general definition of a "financial conglomerate" which could not serve a legislative purpose. This approach would reflect the practice in existing banking and securities legislation. There is no general definition of a 'group of credit institutions' to which the supervision on a consolidated basis applies. Instead, Directive 92/30/EEC defines the scope for each rule separately [8].

The following aims at the definition of those undertakings to which rules on the prevention of double gearing should apply.

Although only tentative, the working definition of financial conglomerate which has been used by the Banking Advisory Committee and the Insurance Committee in the EU could serve as a starting point for the elaboration of a legal definition:

> "A conglomerate is taken to be a group of companies whose activities largely, though not necessarily wholly, consist of providing financial services in different sectors. Such a conglomerate must include at least two of the following three types of supervised - under EC law - financial institutions:

---

[7] The term 'group' is used in this paragraph in order to denote a sample of at least two undertakings which are connected by a certain link. It is not intended to give a legal definition of the term 'group' which is therefore put in inverted commas.

[8] Compare, for instance, the general 'scope' in Article 2, the scope of the exercise of supervision on a consolidated basis in the case of 'groups' in Article 3 (1) and (2) (credit institution and relevant subsidiaries and participations and financial holding companies and their relevant subsidiaries) and the scope of the rules on the access to information in Article 3 (10)

- banks,
- insurance undertakings,
- investment firms."

In a nutshell, this definition would include all elements necessary to distinguish a "financial conglomerate" from other 'groups' of undertakings. The following criteria remain to be discussed:

- The relevant relationship between the undertakings ("group")
- The relevant activities and undertakings ("supervised companies providing financial services"
- The specific composition of the "group" (activities consist "largely, though not necessarily wholly of financial services of at least two different sectors")

2.4.2. THE RELEVANT RELATIONSHIP BETWEEN THE UNDERTAKINGS ("GROUP")

Any approach for a legal definition of a financial conglomerate would need to contain elements defining the relevant *relationship* between the undertakings that form the conglomerate. Existing Community legislation contains many definitions of relationships between undertakings which might also serve as definition of the relevant relationship. The most important are referred to here in order to give an overview and to identify those definitions which appear most suitable in the present context. They are:

- "parent undertaking";
- "subsidiary"; "control";
- "participating interest";
- "participation";
- "close links".

In all three financial services sectors Community legislation contains identical definitions of "parent undertaking" and "subsidiary". These refer to the Seventh Company Law Directive (83/349/EEC) [9].

A slightly different concept of "parent undertaking" and "subsidiary" exists in the context of Directive 92/30/EEC for banking 'groups' (and via the reference in Art. 7 of Directive 93/6/EEC also for investment firm 'groups'). The aforecited definition of parent undertaking in the three sectional directives is extended by "any undertaking which, in the opinion of the competent authorities, effectively exercises a dominant influence over another undertaking". The definition of "subsidi-

---

[9]   c.f. Article 1 (12) and (13) of Directive 89/646/EEC, Article 1 (h) and (i) of Directive 92/49/EEC, Article 1 (i) and (j) of Directive 92/96/EEC and Article 1 (11) and (12) of Directive 93/22/EEC.

ary" is extended in the same way [10]. This extension has notably been made in order to give the competent authorities sufficient discretion to cope with attempts of circumventing supervision on a consolidated basis.

Another closely related concept is that of "control" which can also be found in the directives of all three sectors [11]. This concept refers to the "parent-subsidiary relationship" as defined in Article 1 of Directive 83/349/EEC and extends it to "a similar relationship between any natural or legal person and an undertaking".

Another concept which should be taken into consideration is the "participating interest" or "participation". Again, there are several definitions [12].

The aforecited concepts of "participating interest" and "participation" have a point in common: all of them apply a 20% threshold. The broadest concept of "participation", however, is contained in Directive 92/30/EEC. It contains both direct and indirect holdings of both voting rights and capital. The narrowest concept is the "participating interest" as defined in Article 17 of Directive 78/660/EEC. It is confined to rights in the capital which create a "durable link" and which are intended to contribute to the activities of the company which holds these rights.

The definition of "participation" in the Common Position for the "BCCI Directive" lies somehow between the two other concepts. It includes the direct ownership of capital or voting rights but apparently confines the indirect ownership to those cases where the ownership is mediated by the "way of control". Control, in turn, is defined in the Common Position for the BCCI Directive very close to the 'control' as cited above.

A further relationship which might be of interest is the concept of "close links" (Art. 2 (1) of the Common Position for the "BCCI-Directive"). It combines the alternatives of "control" and "participation" as defined in that text.

Given this choice of possible relevant links, several arguments militate for a logical selection along the lines of the concept used in Directive 92/30/EEC, i.e. choosing the definitions of this Directive of "parent undertaking", "subsidiary" and "participation". Such a choice would give the necessary flexibility and broadness of the scope and would in addition maintain coherence between the supervisory concepts in the different sectors.

---

[10]   c.f. Art. 1 7th and 8th indent of Directive 92/30/EEC.

[11]   c.f. Art. Article 1 (9) of Directive 89/646/EEC, Article 1 (f) of Directive 92/49/EEC, Article 1 (g) of Directive 92/96/EEC and Article 1 (14) of Directive 93/22/EEC.

[12]   Compare Art. 17 of Directive 78/660/EEC and Art. 1, sixth indent of Directive 92/30/EEC and, most recently suggested: Art. 2 (1) (a) of the Common Position (EC No 24/94) for the "BCCI-Directive", OJ No C 213, of 3.8.94, p. 29.

On the other hand, it appears premature to rule out or choose the concept of "close links" because this concept is still under discussion in Parliament and Council.

It appears that the "parent-subsidiary relationship" should in any case be an element of the definition of a financial conglomerate. It also seems to be appropriate to complement this by another element which would be based on a 20%-threshold.

Both elements (the parent-subsidiary relationship and the 'participation' link) contain an aspect of vertical positions in a 'group'. For the sake of clarity and in order to identify the 'positions' of different undertakings within a financial conglomerate, terminology to denote the 'vertical' (and thus *indirectly* also the 'horizontal') relationships appears necessary.

2.4.3. THE RELEVANT ACTIVITIES AND UNDERTAKINGS ("SUPERVISED COMPANIES PROVIDING FINANCIAL SERVICES")

As regards the aspect of the "relevant activities and undertakings" constituting a financial conglomerate, the working definition referred to before could be described in more concrete terms. "Financial services" should comprise the activities of 'credit institutions', 'investment firms' and 'insurance undertakings' (as defined in the Community legislation for the three sectors). All these undertakings are 'supervised undertakings'. It is suggested to define the relevant undertakings according to the definitions given in the existing directives (p.m. this coincides with the definition of 'supervised undertaking' in the document XV/1109/94; however, when this definition will be spelled out in greater detail, the question of whether it encapsulates third country undertakings will have to be clarified; related questions are discussed in the context of the location).

There are, however, two types of undertakings which would not fall under this definition but which should be nevertheless taken into account: certain unsupervised (financial) undertakings and certain holding companies. The exact definition of the 'relevant' unsupervised (financial) undertakings would also require examination. Similarly, a more exact definition of a 'financial conglomerate holding company' must be discussed.

It follows that the presence of "supervised undertakings" shall be a necessary condition for the existence of a conglomerate whereas the presence of unsupervised (financial) undertakings or holding companies would just be a possible additional element.

2.4.4. THE SPECIFIC COMPOSITION OF THE "GROUP" (ACTIVITIES CONSIST "LARGELY, THOUGH NOT NECESSARILY WHOLLY OF FINANCIAL SERVICES OF AT LEAST TWO DIFFERENT SECTORS")

The working definition stresses the fact that the activities must consist "largely though not necessarily wholly of financial services". The rationale for this is that a distinction has to be made between 'financial conglomerates' and 'mixed groups' which contain all kinds of undertakings (commercial or industrial) along with some financial activities. The perception is that the activities of such 'mixed groups' are so heterogeneous that any 'group supervision' would not give a meaningful picture.

This distinction between 'financial groups' and 'mixed groups' has a precedent in existing Community legislation: Directive 92/30/EEC distinguishes between 'financial holding companies' and 'mixed-activity holding companies' (c.f. Article 1). A credit institution (or investment firm) which is a subsidiary of a mixed-activity holding company is not to be supervised on the basis of the consolidated financial situation of the mixed-activity holding company. The criterion to distinguish between a 'financial holding company' and a 'mixed-activity holding company' is the amount of financial activities within the group led by the holding company. The subsidiary undertakings of a financial holding company must be "either exclusively or mainly" credit institutions (investment firms) or financial institutions. On the other hand, the definition of a 'mixed-activity holding company' requires the presence of at least one credit institution (investment firm) subsidiary.

The rationale for the distinction between 'financial groups' and 'mixed-activity groups' made in Directive 92/30/EEC appears to be valid in the financial conglomerate context as well. It is therefore suggested confining the definition of 'financial conglomerate' to 'groups' which are "either exclusively or mainly" active in "financial services".

A second question concerns the *type* of the relevant financial services. In other words, on which basis would one have to calculate the share of 'financial services' present in the 'group'? One could imagine taking into account as 'financial services' the activities of all 'supervised undertakings' and also the activities of any relevant unsupervised undertakings in the group.

It may be worth noting that a similar approach has been chosen for the banking and securities sectors (see the definition of 'financial holding company' which refers to 'credit institutions' and 'financial institutions' as relevant subsidiaries)[13].

---

[13]   Art. 1, third indent of Directive 92/30/EEC.

A third question concerns the composition of the financial conglomerate. The working definition refers to "at least two different financial sectors". Accordingly a 'group' build by a credit institution and its investment firm subsidiary would be a 'financial conglomerate'. The problem which arises here is to draw the correct borderline between a 'financial conglomerate' and those 'groups' which are already covered (or will be covered) by special sectional legislation. The following table explains the relevant cases:

(1)	(2)	(3)	(4)	(5)	(6)
credit institution	credit institution	investment firm	insurance undertaking	credit institution	investment firm
credit institution	investment firm	investment firm	insurance undertaking	insurance undertaking	insurance undertaking

The cases of columns 1 to 3 are already covered by Community legislation [14]. The respective 'groups' come within the scope of supervision on a consolidated basis. Given this situation, it does not seem appropriate to include 'groups' in which credit institutions operate along with investment firms in the definition of a "financial conglomerate". If they were included, confusion on the applicable rules would occur.

As regards 'groups' of insurance undertakings, it is of interest that work is been doing in the European Commission to elaborate appropriate rules for the supervision of insurance 'groups', which includes *inter alia* rules on the prevention of double gearing.

One way to solve the problem raised in chapter 1 is therefore to confine the definition of a "financial conglomerate" to those 'groups' in which at least one insurance undertaking is active along with at least one supervised undertaking of a different sector (cases of columns 5 and 6). For these 'groups' rules on the prevention of double gearing must still be elaborated in EC-law, though.

At the same time, this precision may make it possible to be more specific on the type of holding company which would be a "financial conglomerate holding company". The relevant criterion would be that the holding company has "either exclusively or mainly supervised undertakings and relevant unsupervised undertakings as related undertakings" (difference to the "mixed-activity holding company"). At least one of the related supervised undertakings of the holding company must be an insurance undertaking and at least one must be a supervised undertaking of a sector other than insurance (difference to a "financial holding company" and an "insurance holding company").

---

[14]   Directive 92/30/EEC and 93/6/EEC.

2.5. THE CASE NORWAY BY S. SIMONSEN [15]

2.5.1. BACKGROUND

I would like to start out with the background of our present regulation regarding financial groups. In the Norwegian legislation you will not find the term "conglomerate" but instead the term "group" is used. (For the definition of "group", see the next paragraph (2.5.2.).)

Legal regulation on financial institutions (the term financial institutions refers to banks, financing companies, mortgage companies, insurance companies and holding companies within a financial group) consisted until 1988 of the following acts:

    Insurance Activities Act (1911)
    Act on Commercial Banks (1961)
    Act on Savings Banks (1961)
    Financial Services Act (1976)

(Also the Companies Act (1976) and Act on the Supervision of Credit Institutions, Insurance Companies and Securities Trading etc. (1956 - but totally revised in 1985) are of general importance).

These Acts did not regulate financial groups, and important issues in these laws were not harmonised.

During the mid-1980s, before the banking crisis, the authorities, that is the Ministry of Finance and the Banking, Insurance and Securities Commission (the last one referred to as the supervisory authority), discovered some shortcomings in the regulations. This prompted them to look further into the current legislation.

In 1988 two new important acts were added - the Insurance Activities Act, and the Financial Services Act. The new Insurance Activities Act was a complete modernisation of the earlier Act. The new Insurance Activities Act introduced, with regard to life insurance, several new principles:

-   Accumulated capital shall be distributed annually among the individual contracts.
-   The company shall each year send the policyholder an updated statement of his individual account.
-   The right to transfer the contract from one company to another based on the updated values of the individual contract.

---

[15]   Senior Executive Officer with The Banking, Insurance and Securities Commission of Norway.

With regard to financial groups the Financial Services Act[16] is far more interesting. This Act proved to be very important when it came to creating an equal framework for the activities in financial institutions. It was also important in order to organise a safety net for the institutions itself. The act contains rules regarding all financial institutions (banks, insurance companies, holding companies within a financial group etc.). It thus creates an overall framework for all financial activities, but also includes special regulations for financing companies, and loan intermediairies.

With regard to financial groups the main new elements, compared with the earlier legislation, were:

- The new Financial Services Act contained regulation applicable to all financial institutions - including insurance and holding companies within a financial group. The Insurance Activities Act was drafted in accordance with this regulation and changes were made in the other acts.
- The act introduced a maximum ownership limit for one single owner of 10 per cent in all financial institutions, including holding companies. Exceptions were made for 100% ownership within a group. Other exemptions may be granted.
- Equal capital adequacy rules, which cover the credit risk for all financial institutions, including insurance companies and holding companies, within a financial group. These rules apply to both the individual company and consolidated for the group and for any sub-groups. We use the same rules as in the EU regulations for credit institutions. The credit risk for a given credit engagement/ investment/buying of securities is of course the same independent of the institution giving the credit/making the investment/buying the securities.
- No person who is a board member in a financial institution or has a senior position in a financial institution may concurrently be a board member of another financial institution. Exception exists for companies within a group.

Until December of 1991 a financial group was not allowed to include both a bank and an insurance company at the same time. But in 1991 the legislation was extended with an amendment to the Financial Services Act so as to include also what we refer to as "mixed groups", i.e. a group that includes both a bank and an insurance company. In preparation for this change of regulation we revised the rules regarding financial groups - including the capital adequacy rules.

A Law Committee on Banking is currently looking into all the financial regulation. As far as I know they will propose that all the acts mentioned here will be replaced by one single act. I believe that this Act will be divided in a general part for all financial institutions, including holding companies, with separate specialised parts for banks, insurance companies and other activities.

---

[16] See Appendix 2.1.

2.5.2. DEFINITION OF A FINANCIAL GROUP

In Norway we do not have any significant problems to define a financial group for regulatory or supervisory purposes. We have a legal definition and combined with the other rules few problems arise.

In the Financial Services Act [17] we find the definition of a *"financial group"*:

a "financial group" means groups in which at least one company, which is not the parent company, is a financial institution falling within section 1-4. (Mainly this will be banks, financing companies, mortgage companies, and insurance companies - both life and non-life).

The *group* definition is the same as in the Companies Act - it reads as follows (unofficial translation):

"If a joint stock company owns so many shares or interests in another company that they represent the majority of the votes, the former company will be regarded as parent company and the latter as subsidiary. If a parent company together with a subsidiary, or one or more subsidiaries together own so many shares or interests in another company as mentioned in the preceding sentence, then the latter company also will be regarded as subsidiary of the parent company.

If moreover a joint stock company, as owner of shares or interest or by virtue of agreement, has determining influence over another company and a substantial participation in the result of its operation, then the former company will be regarded as the parent company and the latter as a subsidiary.

A parent company together with its subsidiary or subsidiaries form a company group."

Also companies with close co-operation - like two mutual insurance companies with the same administration, same marketing and other bindings - might be considered a group according to the Financial Services Act. A mere co-operation - like an agreement between a bank and a life insurance company on distribution of insurance products - is however not enough to be considered a group. There has to be more bindings.

An insurance captive in an industrial group is not enough for the whole group to be considered a financial group. Other than captives no bank or insurance company will be a part of an industrial group.

---

[17]   Section 2a-2.

A *mixed group* is defined as:

"a financial group including both a bank and an insurance company".[18]

If there is a holding company in the financial group, then it too is regarded as a financial institution.[19] I.e. ownership limitations, capital adequacy rules, rules regarding posts in controlling bodies and so forth - also apply to the holding company itself.

As mentioned earlier we do not have any significant problems with the distinction on whether it is a financial group or not or if it consists mainly of insurance activities (thus the group should be under supervision from the insurance authorities) or banking activities (banking supervision). There are several reasons for this additional to what is already mentioned:

- Ownership limitations.[20] No single owner - or group of owners either legally connected or assumed to be acting in concert in the exercise of shareholders rights[15] - may hold more than 10 per cent of the shares in a financial institution. Exceptions may be granted - but are quite rarely given if it is not 100 per cent ownership. So usually a company is either inside or outside the group and not somewhere in-between. There is a restriction on voting rights [21] stating that no one can vote for more than 10 per cent of the total number of shares or 20 per cent of the votes represented at the general meeting.[22]
- Organisational restrictions. There are limitations on what companies can be encompassed in a financial group [23], and the authorities must also approve of the organisational structure of the group.[24]
- Supervision. It is regarded as a substantial benefit that we only have one supervisory authority supervising banks, insurance companies, security houses etc. and holding companies in a financial group. With this supervisory structure there are no problems supervising mixed groups, groups on a consolidated basis or the individual company itself.
- Harmonised legislation. As mentioned earlier, the new Financial Services Act harmonised much of the legislation that previously only applied to certain activities. Sweden and Denmark do also have one supervisory authority, but their legislation is not harmonised, as far as I know.

---

[18]   Section 2a-2 b.
[19]   Section 2a-2 d.
[20]   Section 2-2.
[21]   Section 2-6.
[22]   Section 2-4.
[23]   Exceptions exist for ownership within a group and also in accordance with section 2-4.
[24]   See section 2a-6.
[25]   See section 2a-7.

-   Consolidation. For solvency purposes we require consolidation of ownership exceeding 20 per cent.[26]

2.5.3. ORGANISATION

For mixed groups there are two possible ways of organising the group[27]:

-   A holding company on top with a bank subsidiary and an insurance subsidiary (all companies may themselves own other companies in accordance with the legislation for banks or insurance companies). This model should be used if both the bank and the insurance company are limited companies.
-   A bank may own an insurance subsidiary through a wholly owned holding company. Or an insurance company may own a bank subsidiary through a wholly owned holding company. Again all the companies can have their own subsidiaries. This model is used if a savings bank or a mutual insurance company is involved. It has also been used if one of the companies is substantially larger than the other.

The reason for this set up is to create "fire walls" between the companies in order to avoid one company subsidising another. We feel that this is especially important if an insurance company is involved in a group.

2.5.4. CONCURRENT POSITIONS IN BOARDS

Up until 1988 we registered that the same persons were sitting in controlling bodies of several financial institutions at the same time. The decisions, not only in the financial market, but also in industrial companies, were made by a few - hopefully good - men. These people were referred to, at least by some, as the "gentlemen's club". In financial groups the boards of the subsidiaries usually only consist of people employed by the group or persons who held other positions in the controlling bodies of the group. This could lead to situations where the board members do not make decisions that will prove to be the best for the financial institutions, but make decisions that are influenced by what is in the interest of the other companies where they are employed or where they are board members (within or outside the group).

According to the Act of 1988[28] it is prohibited for a person being board member of a financial institution or holding a senior position in a financial institution to be a board member of another financial institution at the same time, unless this is approved by the authorities.

---

[26] See section 2a-9 and other regulation in accordance with this section.
[27] See section 2-2 no 1 and 2 in the Financial Services Act
[28] Section 2-8 and regulation in accordance with this section.

For subsidiaries within a financial group there is a general exception for up to three quarters of the number of board members. But the final quarter cannot hold any position as a board member in a financial institution, nor be employed by the group or by any other financial institution. Outside the group anyone who wants to hold more than one of the positions mentioned needs an individual permit in each particular case.

We have however discovered some weaknesses in the regulation. Quite often the managing director in the mother company is the chairman of all the subsidiaries in the group. This might in some situations lead to a conflict of interest where the general good of one company is sacrificed for the benefit of another. The Law Committee on Banking is looking into this problem.

2.5.5. TRANSACTIONS BETWEEN COMPANIES (ENTERPRISES) IN A FINANCIAL GROUP

A very important principle in the regulation concerning financial groups is that we treat each company separately at the same time as we acknowledge it as a part of a group. In order to protect the individual company we have certain rules regarding transactions between the companies in a group.[29]

Transactions between enterprises in a financial group shall be in accordance with ordinary business terms and principles. This is a general principle for all transactions within a financial group. There shall be no cross-subsidising - no sales below market value, and no transaction which only or mainly benefits one company. The supervisory authority may order changes in case transactions are not in accordance with this provision. In some cases we have demanded a reversal of such transactions.

Our largest insurance holding company, UNI Storebrand, tried - hours before it came under public administration - to sell some real estate to its life insurance subsidiary. The price and other terms were in accordance with marked terms - but not the situation itself. The life insurance company had not had the opportunity to decide for itself if this was a transaction they wanted to enter into or not. It was only decided by the mother company in order to help the mother company. The transaction was therefore not approved by the supervisory authority. (By the way - this transaction would probably not have been sufficient to avoid the liquidity crisis that the mother company entered into - merely postpone it).

A financial group shall have internal rules for its activity which ensure that revenues, expenses, losses and gains are distributed as correctly as possible among the group enterprises and among the group areas of activity. The supervisory

[29]   See section 2a-8.

authority shall supervise such distribution and may order changes to be made in transactions among the group enterprises or changes to be made in other dispositions which have brought about a distribution that is not in accordance with the principles set out in this rule. The supervisory authority may issue further rules on such distribution, which we have not done so far.

Contributions within a group may not be given by one sister company to another. The link between sister companies originates in the mother company;- thus contributions must follow the same path. Contributions together with dividends, must not exceed a prudent distribution of dividend based on the individual year's operation unless the King (government), in order to secure the financial strength of a group company, authorises a higher contribution.

A group company may only make loans to or provide guarantees in favour of another company within the group if it is within the restrictions of credit to one single customer. The companies in a group are consolidated. Holding companies and a mother company if it is a bank, may exceed this credit limit if a permission is granted by the supervisory authority. Insurance companies may not, under any circumstances, make any loans or provide guarantees in favour of another company within the group. This is to prevent that policyholder's fund be diverted to other companies within the group.

Appendix 2.A.

(Legislation of Norway)

Act no. 40 of 10 June 1988 on Financing Activity and Financial Institutions (Financial Services Act) as amended, last by Act no. 76 of 11 June 1993

A.1. FINANCIAL INSTITUTIONS

Section 2-1   Scope
The provisions of this chapter apply to financial institutions. A company or other institution that is the parent company in a financial group or the parent company in part of such group is also regarded as a financial institution.

A.1.1. OWNERSHIP STRUCTURE, ETC.

Section 2-2   Holdings in financial institutions
No-one may hold more than 10 per cent of the share capital in a financial institution. A financial institution may nonetheless hold up to 20 per cent of the share capital in a finance company or mortgage company, loan intermediary or credit-insurance enterprise providing the enterprise has been authorised to carry on, or has commenced, such activity prior to 1 January 1987.

The restrictions of the first paragraph do not prevent

- an insurance company from being 100 per cent owned by
    * a parent company in a group or jointly by several companies within a group, provided that the distribution of shares in the parent company is in accordance with the restrictions on holdings set out in section 2-2, first paragraph and section 2-3, cf. section 2-6, or by
    * a mutual insurance company or mutual insurance companies which through co-operation agreements form a group entity based on joint controlling bodies which are provided for in their articles of association, cf. Act on Insurance Activity, section 4-10.
    * a bank, provided the bank owns the company through a wholly-owned subsidiary which pursuant to its articles of association shall not engage in other activity than administering its holdings in insurance companies.
- a bank from being 100 per cent owned by
    * a parent company in a group that falls within the Act on Insurance Activity or a parent company which pursuant to its articles of association shall not engage in other activity than administering its holdings in financial groups;

cf. section 2a-2, litera b), provided that the distribution of shares is in accordance with the restrictions on holdings set out in section 2-2, first paragraph, and section 2-3, cf. section 2-6, or by

* an insurance company, or a group entity as mentioned in section 4-10 in the Act on Insurance Activity, or similar group entity approved by the Ministry of Finance, provided that the bank is 100 per cent owned through a subsidiary which pursuant to its articles of association shall not engage in other activity than administering its holdings in companies which do not engage in insurance activities.

- a finance or mortgage company or loan intermediary from being owned 100 per cent by a bank or an insurance company or jointly by companies within the group of which the bank or insurance company forms part, or by a group entity as mentioned in section 4-10 of the Act on Insurance Activity or a similar group entity approved by the Ministry of Finance, or a finance or mortgage company or loan intermediary from being 100 per cent owned by a mortgage company.

- a finance or mortgage company or loan intermediary from being 100 per cent owned by another finance or mortgage company which according to its articles of association shall not carry on other activity than administering its holdings in financial institutions.

- a credit insurance company from being 100 per cent owned by a bank or jointly by companies within the group of which the bank forms part.

- a foreign financial institution from having a subsidiary established in Norway with authorisation from the King.

- the Government Bank Insurance Fund and the Government Bank Investment Fund from owning more than 10 per cent of the share capital in Norwegian banks.

- two or more financial institutions from together owning, with the King's consent, 100 per cent of another financial institution which pursuant to its articles of association shall offer special financial services.

- the King may in special cases make exceptions from the restrictions on holdings in the first paragraph.

In the event of conversion of financial institutions pursuant to sections 2-18 to 2-24, the provisions of the first and second paragraphs do not apply for the foundation's acquisition of holdings in the converted institution or the parent company of the institution.

Section 2-3   Holdings of non-Norwegian citizens

No-one who is not a Norwegian citizen may own more than 10 per cent of the share capital in a financial institution. In the case of companies with non-voting shares or shares with restricted voting power, persons who are not Norwegian citizens may in no event own shares which altogether represent more than 10 per cent of the votes in the company. The King may in special cases make exceptions to the restrictions on holdings set out in the first and second sentence.

Non-Norwegian citizens may altogether own shares representing up to 33.33 per cent of the share capital in a financial institution. In the case of companies with non-voting shares or shares with restricted voting power, non-Norwegian citizens may in no event own shares which altogether represent more than 33.33 per cent of the votes in the company.

If the restriction on the overall holding or voting power of non-Norwegian citizens is exceeded, the necessary reduction shall be made such that earlier share acquisitions rank ahead of recent ones.

Equivalent to Norwegian citizens for the purpose of this section are the Norwegian state, institutions and funds that are controlled by the state, Norwegian municipalities, Norwegian banks, corporations and foundations with a board of which a majority, including the chairman, are Norwegian citizens, and with their head offices in Norway and whose purpose is to benefit the public good, as well as joint stock companies and other companies with limited liability with a board of which a majority, including the chairman, are Norwegian citizens, and with their head offices in Norway when at least two-thirds of their primary capital belongs to the state, Norwegian municipalities or Norwegian citizens. Companies in which shares or interests representing more than one half of the votes are held by the state, municipality or county municipality shall in all circumstances be considered equivalent to Norwegian citizens.

This section does not apply to shares held in a financial institution which is a subsidiary of a foreign financial institution and which has been established in Norway with authorisation from the King.

The restrictions set out in section 2-2, first paragraph, first sentence, and in the first paragraph of this section do not apply to interests in Samvirkegruppen A/S that are held by a foreign interest organisation forming part of a trade union movement, a cooperative organisation or company which is a subsidiary of such an organisation. In case of doubt the King decides whether an organisation or a company falls within this section.

Section 2-4   Restrictions on voting rights
No-one at the general meeting of a financial institution may cast votes for more than 10 per cent of the voting shares in the company or for more than 20 per cent of the voting shares represented at the general meeting. In cases where, in accordance

with section 2-2, first paragraph, a financial institution owns more than 10 per cent of the share capital, it may nonetheless only cast votes for up to 10 per cent of the voting shares in the company.

The rules of this section do not apply at the general meeting of financial institutions that fall within the provisions of section 2-2, second paragraph. The King may decide that the rules of the preceding paragraph shall not apply at the general meeting of a financial institution where the King has made exceptions from restrictions on holdings pursuant to section 2-3, first paragraph, third sentence.

Section 2-5   Underwriting of share issues
No-one may underwrite a share issue if such underwriting could lead to acquisition of shares in excess of the limits set out in sections 2-2 and 2-3.

A financial institution may not underwrite a share issue if such underwriting could lead to acquisition of shares in excess of the limit prescribed by law for the institution's aggregate holdings in other companies.

Section 2-6   Consolidation of holdings
For the purpose of sections 2-2, 2-3, 2-4 and 2-5, first paragraph, shares held or acquired by the following persons and institutions are considered equivalent to the shareholder's own shares:

- the shareholder's spouse, under-age children or persons with whom the share holder shares a household,
- a company in which the shareholder exercises influence as referred to in section 1-2 of the Companies Act,
- a company within the same group as the shareholder, and
- someone with whom the shareholder must be assumed to be acting in concert in the exercise of shareholder rights.

In cases of doubt the King decides whether shares not held by the shareholder shall be considered equivalent to the shareholder's own shares pursuant to the rules of the first paragraph.

Section 2-7   Co-operation agreements
Cooperation agreements between financial institutions which are not part of the same group shall be approved by the Ministry. This does not apply to agreements on individual projects or on technical or practical matters with no significant bearing on competitive conditions.

"Financial institutions" also means securities houses and estate agencies, as well as enterprises which administer unit trusts.

In cases of doubt the King decides whether an agreement requires approval pursuant to the first paragraph.

Section 2-8   Posts in controlling bodies

Unless otherwise decided by the King, no person who is a member of a controlling body or has a senior position in a financial institution may concurrently be a member of a controlling body of another financial institution.

The King issues further rules on the implementation and variation of the prohibition of the first paragraph.

A.1.2. GENERAL RULES FOR BUSINESS

Section 2-9   Capital adequacy requirements

A financial institution shall maintain a satisfactory capital ratio at all times, and meet the minimum capital requirement ensuing from law or regulation issued by the King.

The King may by regulation lay down further rules for the method of calculation and other factors relating to implementation of the capital requirement.

The King may lay down rules to the effect that a financial institution shall also maintain a minimum capital ratio in respect of off-balance-sheet commitments.

A.2.   FINANCIAL GROUPS

Section 2a-1   Scope, etc.

The provisions of this chapter apply to financial groups and their activity unless otherwise provided in provisions in or pursuant to law.

Further rules on financial groups, the parent company in a financial group or in a part of such group, and their activity may be laid down by regulation issued by the King.

Section 2a-2   Definitions

Definitions:

- In this chapter "financial group" means groups in which at least one company, which is not the parent company, is a financial institution falling within section 1-4.
- In this chapter "mixed group" means a financial group including both a bank and an insurance company.
- In this chapter "sub-group" means two or more companies between which a

group relationship exists. The parent company in a financial group does not form part of a subgroup.

- In this chapter "financial institution" also means a company which is only the parent company in a financial group or in a part thereof and whose activity is confined to administering its holdings in the group.

A.2.1. LICENCE

Section 2a-3 Licence requirement etc.

A financial institution which is a parent company as mentioned in section 2a-2, litera d), may not be established without authorisation from the King.

Except when so authorised by the King, a financial institution may not, through establishment or other acquisition, hold interests in another financial institution that are so large that a group relationship exists between the two institutions. Securities houses and estate agencies as well as enterprises which administer unit trusts are also regarded as financial institutions. The taking over of a substantial part of the activity of a financial institution is also regarded as acquisition.

Except when so authorised by the King, a financial institution may not establish a subsidiary or branch abroad or acquire more than 10 per cent of the shares in a foreign financial institution.

Section 2-6 applies pari passu for establishment or acquisition pursuant to the second and third paragraph.

The King may attach conditions to authorisation as mentioned under the first, second and third paragraphs. A condition may be attached to the effect that the activity of the group or enterprises which form part thereof is organised in a particular manner or is operated subject to certain constraints or that certain types of activity may not be engaged in. Other conditions may also be attached in accordance with the interests that the legislation on financial institutions shall promote.

Section 2a-4 Application for licence

Licence applications pursuant to section 2a-3 shall contain such information as is considered to be of significance for processing the applications. In the event of the establishment or acquisition of a financial institution, the licence applicant shall enclose articles of association or draft articles of association and an operating schedule for the first three years of operation of the group. The operating schedule should contain:

- information about the group's corporate structure after the establishment or acquisition,

- an overview of the operating set-up and routines for the business and services that the various enterprises will offer,
- information about the group's capital composition,
- budgets for establishment and administrative costs,
- budgets including the profit and loss account, balance sheet and funds flow statement for each of the first three years, and
- a forecast of the financial position for each of the first three years.

A.2.2. ORGANISATIONAL SET-UP

Section 2a-5   Parent company in a financial group

Subject to the restrictions set out in section 2-2, second paragraph, the parent company in a financial group may be:

- a financial institution falling within section 1-4, or
- a company falling within section 2a-2, litera d).

Section 2a-6   Companies which may form part of a financial group

Unless otherwise provided by law, a financial group may, in addition to a parent company as mentioned in section 2a-5, encompass:

- financial institutions,
- management companies for unit trusts,
- property and investment companies,
- debt collection companies,
- companies which intermediate financial services, and
- companies with a natural connection with financing activity or insurance business.

The organisational set-up of a financial group shall be approved by the King. In connection with such approval, conditions may be attached to the effect that a company, which forms part of a financial group, shall be directly owned by the parent company or be organised in the same sub-group. Special rules apply for the organisational set-up of mixed groups; cf. section 2-2, second paragraph.

Enterprises which intermediate financial services shall be organised in such a way as to secure their status as independent intermediaries as effectively as possible.

Special rules laid down in or pursuant to the Act on Insurance Activity apply for enterprises carrying on insurance business.

The name of the parent company, group unit or the group shall be clear from the name or from an addition to the name of any enterprise that forms part of a financial group when such a group is Norwegian.

Section 2a-7 Changes in organisational set-up

The parent company in a financial group is required to notify the Banking, Insurance and Securities Commission of the following changes in the organisational set-up of the group:

- disposal of holdings as mentioned under section 2a-3, third paragraph, in a financial institution,
- disposal of a subsidiary in a financial group that does not fall within section 2a-3, second paragraph. The provision applies pari passu in the event of disposal of a substantial portion of the activity to a subsidiary,
- closure of a foreign branch.

Changes in organisational set-up other than those mentioned in the first paragraph shall be approved by the King. The King may issue further rules to the effect that changes falling within the notification requirement pursuant to the first paragraph shall be subject to a licensing requirement.

A.2.3. TRANSACTIONS AND CONSOLIDATION

Section 2a-8 Transactions between enterprises in a financial group

Transactions between enterprises in a financial group shall be in accordance with ordinary business terms and principles. The Banking, Insurance and Securities Commission may order that changes be made in transactions between enterprises in the group that are not in accordance with the provision of the first sentence.

A financial group shall have rules for its activity that ensure that revenues, expenses, losses and gains are distributed as correctly as possible among the group enterprises and among the group areas of activity. The Banking, Insurance and Securities Commission shall supervise such distribution and may order that changes be made in transactions among the group enterprises or that changes be made in other dispositions which have brought about a distribution that is not in accordance with the principles set out in the first sentence of this paragraph. The Banking, Insurance and Securities Commission may issue further rules on such distribution.

Group contributions may not be given between sister companies. Nor may group contributions be given by life insurance companies, unless otherwise provided in the company's articles of association. The contribution together with dividend must not exceed a prudent distribution of dividend based on the individual year's operation unless the King, in order to secure the financial strength of a group company, authorises a higher contribution. The King may establish supplementary rules pursuant to this paragraph.

Unless otherwise provided by the King, a group company may not make loans to or provide guarantees in favour of another company within the group.

Unless otherwise provided in the terms of the licence, a securities house which forms part of the group may transact business on behalf of another enterprise in the group. In cases where such broking is performed, the enterprise shall ensure that the opposite party employs a broker unless the terms of the licence state that this is not required.

Section 2a-9   Rules of consolidation

A financial institution shall, when applying rules on capital adequacy and other rules as to financial strength and safety, undertake consolidation pursuant to the rules of this section when it directly or indirectly has a holding which represents 20 per cent or more of the share capital or the votes in:

- another Norwegian or foreign financial institution,
- a Norwegian or foreign securities house, commercial property or property company, investment trust company or other company with substantial financial assets.

The obligation to undertake consolidation also applies to a financial institution which is the parent company in a sub-group, as well as to collaborative mutual insurance companies and other corresponding group affiliates which are not part of an ownership hierarchy.

Group accounts shall be based on the principle of proportional consolidation. The Banking, Insurance and Securities Commission may also instruct consolidation to be implemented in respect of holdings of 10 per cent and more.
In cases where consolidation is not implemented pursuant to the first paragraph, a reserve of 100 per cent of book value shall be set aside in respect of holdings of 10 per cent or more. The Banking, Insurance and Securities Commission may also instruct the financial institution in question to maintain such reserve in respect of holdings of less than 10 per cent.

If a financial institution has invested capital apart from share capital in another financial institution, which alone or together with a holding in the financial institution corresponds to 10 per cent or more of the latter's total capital, and consolidation pursuant to the first paragraph is not effected, a reserve shall be set aside corresponding to 100 per cent of the book value. The Banking, Insurance and Securities Commission may also instruct a financial institution to set aside such reserve when its total capital as mentioned in the first sentence constitutes less than 10 per cent. The King may in special cases grant exception from the provisions of this paragraph.

The Banking, Insurance and Securities Commission may issue further rules concerning the implementation of consolidation or allocation to a capital adequacy reserve pursuant to this section.

3. Application of the most relevant definitions to the relational database

K. Verweire
Erasmus Finance & Insurance Centre (NL)
De Vlerick School voor Management (B)

Some of the definitions of a "financial conglomerate" analysed in chapter 1, will be applied in this chapter. This statistical analysis is based on a database developed within the EFIC (Erasmus Finance & Insurance Centre). We have collected some financial data to measure the economic impact of the "all finance" movement in the European Union.

At the start of this study, the focus was to collect all relevant information to set up a "complete" database on "all" types of financial conglomerates.
Due to the rather innovative character of the formation of financial conglomerates, there is a lack of clear definitions and no reliable complete reference basis exists. Consequently, a great deal of time and energy went into the development of a vast inventory of "potential relevant institutions". The establishment of a useful method to set up the relational database also took quite a long time[1].

The collection and analysis of financial data[2] could only start after we had a better view on the relevant financial groups. Consequently, the first aspect - the testing of the different definitions - is, for the moment, the most important part of this chapter.

Neither the financial statistics, nor the inventory of financial conglomerates are therefore complete nor accurate for the moment. Nevertheless, the database is large enough to make some interesting analyses.

---

[1] The development of the database was carried out by Jaap van der Veen, education assistant and responsible for the information network of the Erasmus Finance & Insurance Centre.

[2] A great part of the collection and the analysis of financial data was done by Marco Scheffers, former research assistant at the Erasmus Finance & Insurance Centre.

3.1.   **THE COLLECTION OF THE DATA**

The first question that arose was how to test the different definitions of a financial conglomerate.

There are two important elements in defining a financial conglomerate:

- it relates to a group of enterprises;
- it is a combination of different kinds of financial institutions.

In one way or another, these two elements should be involved in our testing process.

Perhaps, it's better to look first at the basic structure of the database. We have opted for a relational database in view of the complexity of the problem. The most important advantage of a relational database is the possibility to build different parts when appropriate. The only thing you have to take care of, is to link the different parts of the database.

We built our "financial conglomerates" database around two parts:

- a "company" part;
- a "relations between companies" part.

These parts are databases themselves, but they can easily be combined to be able to get answers on very specific questions.

In the future, the purpose is to build other "databases" in extension of what we already have: e.g. a database "financial data" or a database "persons" (to examine interlocking directorships).

In the "company" database all relevant data about the company is stored:

- the name of the enterprise;
- the country of the head office;
- the activity of the enterprise.

This last topic is very interesting for our study because we want to be able to observe what types of companies and services or activities are part of a financial conglomerate. First we made a distinction between a holding, an insurance institution, a credit institution, an investment institution and a rest category, named "unspecified".

But after a certain time, we were compelled to break up the categorie "holding" into several subcategories, namely "insurance holding" (e.g. ING Verzekeringen), "credit holding" (e.g. Compagnie financière de CIC et de l'Union Européenne), "mixed holding" (e.g. ING Group, ASLK-Group) and "other holding" (non-financial holdings).

In the other database "relations (between companies)", we stored all the data about relations between the financial institutions. We noted:

- the type of relation: a "participation" or just a "co-operation";
- the companies involved;
- if the relation was a participation, we collected the percentage; however, it's true that the percentage of stocks owned by a company is not the complete answer to the question whether the companies can be seen as a group or not, but anyhow, it's a first step;
- information on the type and the date of publication of the sources used.

The data collection of participations was - and still is - a very difficult part of the study, because we couldn't always find the necessary information. Problems we frequently met were the following:

- Sometimes we couldn't find the exact company of the group who has taken a holding in another company; e.g. "UAP has taken over Nieuw Rotterdam" meant in fact that "UAP International" has a controlling stake in "Vinci BV" which has in turn a controlling stake in "Nieuw Rotterdam".
  Yet, the further we went, the more the pieces of the puzzle fitted. However, there are still some missing links in the database.
- Often, the exact percentage of the holding was omitted. How big is a "substantial holding" ? (We have defined it as a participation between 20 and 50 %[3], but did the journalist of the Financial Times use the same criterion ?).
- Rarely (but it happened), the information was totally wrong.

These problems, together with the fact that we, here in the Benelux, couldn't always acquire information about movements in for instance Greece or Portugal, are the reason why this database is certainly not complete.

However, we hope we can complete this database so it becomes an appropriate tool for a more thorough analysis of different aspects of "financial conglomerates".

In this context, it is important to notice that the results we have gathered must be seen as just an indication of what is really going on; it does certainly not pretend to be a thorough and complete analysis of financial conglomerates in the EU.

---

[3]   It must be emphasized that also a 20% and a 50% participation are to be considered as substantial holdings.

3.2. **THE RESULTS**

The results of the analysis we've carried out on the database are summarized in some tables.

3.2.1. DEFINING THE TYPE AND NUMBER OF FINANCIAL CONGLOMERATES

The first thing we wanted to know was the number of "financial conglomerates" that could be detected from our database.

You can find the results in table 3.1.
For each country of the EU, the total number of companies ("Companies") is given.
The next column ("Qualified institution") gives the number of companies which comply with the following criteria:

- The company is a credit institution (or credit holding), an insurance institution (or insurance holding) or a mixed holding,
- and has at least a 5 % stake in a company of the other type (e.g. a credit institution has a holding of 10 % in an insurance company, ...).

The fourth column ("Financial conglomerate") contains the number of groups that comply with the criteria mentioned above.
The difference between the third and the fourth column lies in the fact that in a group (e.g. the ING Group) different companies can meet the criterion as mentioned above e.g. "Nationale Nederlanden", the big insurance company of the group has a stake of almost 100 % in "Westland-Utrecht Hypotheekbank", a credit instition in the ING Group; but "De Vaderlandsche", one of the Belgian insurance daughters, also meets the criterion (it has a stake of 100 % in "De Vaderlandsche Spaarbank", a Belgian saving bank). In the third column, "Nationale Nederlanden" as well as "De Vaderlandsche" are taken into account, while in the next column the ING Group counts for only one unit.
In the last column, you find some figures published by the CEA[4] in a special issue of July 1993. They considered only participations of more than 10 % to determine the number of financial conglomerates (while we used 5 %) and they also involved investment and other non-financial institutions in their analysis (while we didn't).

---

[4]   Comité Européen des Assurances - Special Issue N°1 - July 1993 - "Financial Conglomerates".

Table 3.1: Overview of the database and comparison with CEA figures.

Country	Companies	Qualified institution	Financial conglom.	CEA figures
Belgium	387	25	14	?
Denmark	40	3	3	6
France	238	28	22	24
Germany	137	10	9	>11
Great Britain	149	7	7	44
Greece	10	0	0	8
Ireland	21	2	2	4
Italy	81	6	4	±30
Luxemburg	70	2	1	4
Netherlands	753	25	13	12
Portugal	26	5	4	14
Spain	95	8	6	28
Total EU	2007	121	85	185
Rest	523	20	18	?
Total	2530	141	103	?

There are 2.530 companies in the database of which 80 % are EU companies. We have found 121 EU companies complying with the criteria: participation in another type of enterprise and a participation of more than 5 %.

These 121 enterprises belonged to 85 groups (financial conglomerates). The largest share of those companies comes from France, the Netherlands and Belgium. This is probably due to the fact that we had more information about those countries.

There is a vast difference between the CEA figures and the figures of our study on EU level: we have found 85 "financial conglomerates" while the CEA speaks of 185 "financial conglomerates", Belgium not included.

Another source[5] mentioned about 200 financial conglomerates in the EU. One possible reason for this is that the CEA has taken a greater scope: they have also involved investment and other non-financial institutions. Furthermore, they considered groups with only one regulated financial undertaking as a financial conglomerate[6].

Despite all these remarks, in the Netherlands and the neighbouring countries

---

[5] Wilko H. BÖRNER, Chairman of the Management Board of "Volksfürsorge" mentioned the following at a conference of CAPA/EFMA : "FINANZKONGLOMERATE ...Allein in der EG gibt es bereits 200 solche Konzerne". (Conference Paper CAPA/EFMA : "Die Überwachung der Finanz-konglomerate aus der sicht eines Deutschen Versicherer", 1993, pp 267-288).

[6] CEA (1993): "Eg., conglomerates comprising one financial undertaking and one industrial under-taking; group comprising an insurance company and a broking company ..."

(France, Germany and probably Belgium too; Great Britain is an exception) our figures come close to those of the CEA. Underrepresented are probably the groups from Great Britain, Italy, Spain and Greece.

We have found only 85 financial conglomerates because our requirements were very strict. In cases where we couldn't obtain the exact percentage of the participation, we didn't mention this company in the list "Qualified institution" and consequently not in the list "Financial conglomerate".
We made the little exercise to look at the companies who had a participation in the other type of enterprise and of which the percentage of the participation was unknown. This share could be 2 % or 99 % but we think that for most of the companies, this share is quite substantial. If we add these figures to the figures we already have from table 3.1, we obtain the figures of table 3.2.

We found 21 additional companies (qualified institutions) for the EU: 6 in Great Britain, 4 in France, 3 in Italy, 2 in Germany and 1 in Spain, Luxemburg, Ireland, Portugal, Denmark and the Netherlands. This resulted in 16 additional financial conglomerates for the EU.
Furthermore, we found 7 Austrian, 1 American, 1 Swedish and 1 Finnish potential conglomerate(s).

Table 3.2: Overview of the database and comparison with CEA figures (completed with the unknown figures)

Country	Companies	Qualified institution	Financial conglom.	CEA figures
Belgium	387	25	14	?
Denmark	40	4	4	6
France	238	32	26	24
Germany	137	12	10	>11
Great Britain	149	13	11	44
Greece	10	0	0	8
Ireland	21	3	3	4
Italy	81	9	7	±30
Luxemburg	70	3	2	4
Netherlands	753	26	13	12
Portugal	26	6	5	14
Spain	95	9	6	28
Total EU	2007	142	101	185
Rest	523	30	28	?
Total	2530	172	129	?

In a second phase (table 3.3 - 3.5), we examined the column "Qualified institution" more in detail.

We made two kinds of division.

First, we made a division according to the type of the "active company" (i.e. the company who owns the other company; the company that is "owned" is called the "passive company"). In this way, there are 3 possibilities:

- a credit institution (or holding) has a stake in an insurance institution (or holding);
- an insurance institution (or holding) has a stake in a credit institution (or holding);
- a mixed holding has a stake in a credit and an insurance institution (or holding).

Secondly, we also introduced the percentages of the participation in the following table. We have made a distinction between 5, 20 and 50 % (these percentages are used to define "minor stake", "substantial stake" and "mother/daughter relationship" - see chapter 1).

Table 3.3: Detailed overview of the column "Qualified institution" - comparison at the 5 % level.

Country	Total	Credit → Insurance	Insurance → Credit	Mixed holding
Belgium	25	8	15	2
Denmark	3	1	2	0
France	28	12	16	0
Germany	10	7	3	0
Great Britain	7	5	2	0
Greece	0	0	0	0
Ireland	2	1	1	0
Italy	6	4	2	0
Luxemburg	2	2	0	0
Netherlands	25	6	17	2
Portugal	5	3	2	0
Spain	8	6	1	1
Total EU	121	55	61	5
Rest	20	9	9	2
Total	141	64	70	7

There were 141 credit and insurance institutions or mixed holdings who had a participation of over 5 % in the other kind of enterprise. In the total EU, we had 121 companies, meeting the requirements.

There are more insurance companies having a holding in a credit institution than there are banks with a holding in an insurance institution, however there's little difference (and probably not significant). Therefore, it makes no sense to talk about these findings on EU level. Perhaps, if we have a more complete database, this difference will become significant.

It's better to look at the differences between the countries. In Belgium, Denmark, France and the Netherlands, there are more insurance companies having a stake in a credit institution than vice versa.

On the contrary, in Germany, Great Britain, Italy, Luxemburg, Portugal and Spain, we found the opposite.

We also made a detailed overview at the 20 % (table 3.4) and the 50 % level (table 3.5).

Table 3.4: Detailed overview of the column "Qualified institution" - comparison at the 20 % level.

Country	Total	Credit → Insurance	Insurance → Credit	Mixed holding
Belgium	20	7	11	2
Denmark	3	1	2	0
France	27	12	15	0
Germany	7	4	3	0
Great Britain	6	5	1	0
Greece	0	0	0	0
Ireland	1	1	0	0
Italy	4	3	1	0
Luxemburg	2	2	0	0
Netherlands	23	6	15	2
Portugal	3	3	0	0
Spain	8	6	1	1
Total EU	104	50	49	5
Rest	15	6	7	2
Total	119	56	56	7

There is one thing remarkable in comparison with table 3.3 (5 % level). If we look at EU level, then we see a sharp drop-off in the number of insurance institutions, having a stake in a credit institution of more than 20 %: the number dropped from 61 to 49 (i.e. -12) while this figure for the credit institutions with a participation of more than 20 % in an insurance institution was only 5.

From these figures, we can conclude that the participations of a credit institution in an insurance institution have a more strategic character than is the case with the insurance institutions, having a stake in a credit institution.

Perhaps, the reason for this lies in the fact that insurance institutions are institutional investors while credit institutions are not. Institutional investors sometimes take substantial shareholdings because it is economically interesting (interesting investment, great profit expectations, better fiscal character, ...); this isn't the case with financial intermediaries such as credit institutions: a substantial participation has more the character of a strategical decision.

At the level of the individual countries, there are no significant differences with the former table: Belgium, Denmark, France and the Netherlands are the countries where there are more "active" insurance companies, while in all the other countries (except Greece) there are more "active" credit institutions.

When we compare table 3.4 and 3.5, we observe the opposite phenomenon. Here, the number of credit institutions with majority participations in the insurance sector has been subject to a sharp drop-off, while this is not the case with the insurance companies having a "credit daughter". Remarkable is that this sharp drop-off is due to a decrease of "credit mothers" in almost every EU country. A good example of this trend is Germany, but also Belgium and France are confronted with the same phenomenon. Also remarkable is that in these countries, we notice an important decrease in the number of insurance companies having a stake in credit institutions.

Table 3.5: Detailed overview of the column "Qualified institution" - comparison at the 50 % level.

Country	Total	Credit → Insurance	Insurance → Credit	Mixed holding
Belgium	14	4	9	1
Denmark	3	1	2	0
France	22	9	13	0
Germany	2	2	0	0
Great Britain	6	5	1	0
Greece	0	0	0	0
Ireland	1	1	0	0
Italy	2	1	1	0
Luxemburg	0	0	0	0
Netherlands	23	6	15	2
Portugal	3	3	0	0
Spain	6	4	1	1
Total EU	82	36	42	4
Rest	11	4	5	2
Total	93	40	47	6

3.2.2. ECONOMIC IMPACT OF THE FINANCIAL CONGLOMERATES: SOME ESTIMATIONS

We have collected the financial data on group level for the financial conglomerates within the EU. We had data of 77 financial conglomerates (remember the 101 (possible) financial conglomerates we have found in our database - see table 3.2).

All figures are in mln. ECU. We used the exchange rates of end of October 1992.

In the tables 3.6, 3.7 and 3.8, we show the biggest conglomerates with some key figures: total income[7], balance sheet total and number of employees (figures of 1992). We made a distinction between conglomerates with a primarily insurance character, conglomerates with a primarily banking character and mixed holdings (almost equal parts of insurance and "banking" activities).

The figures are consolidated figures: the problem is that e.g. for insurance institutions also the banking figures are taken into account which is the reason for AXA to be nominated the second largest "insurance conglomerate" before UAP, normally the second largest insurer of Europe.

The same rules apply to the credit institutions: in their figures also the figures of the insurance companies are taken into account.

Therefore, these figures should be considered as an indication of the relative importance of the whole financial conglomeration movement and one should not use these figures for other purposes.

We have tried to collect both "insurance figures" and "banking figures" to give a better insight into this problem, but despite the fact that some conglomerates have made serious efforts, we couldn't always find a clear distinction between banking and insurance figures.

---

[7]   We have defined "total income" as : premium income (direct) + interest income + other operating income.

Table 3.6: Overview of the financial data: the biggest "conglomerates" by total income (1992).

Conglomerate	Country	Insurance conglom.	Credit conglom.	Mixed holding	Absolute figure (mln ECU)	%
1. **Allianz**	D	1			36.714,8	6,6
2. **AXA**	F	2			26.960,7	4,9
3. **UAP**	F	3			25.814,3	4,6
4. **Crédit Lyonnais**	F		1		24.732,0	4,4
5. **Deutsche Bank**	D		2		24.261,2	4,4
6. **Crédit Agricole**	F		3		23.540,1	4,2
7. **ING**	NL			1	22.121,8	4,0
8. **GAN**	F	4			19.598,1	3,5
9. **Banque Paribas**	F		4		18.251,2	3,3
10. **Generali**	I	5			14.804,0	2,7
11. **Dresdner Bank**	D		5		14.677,3	2,6
12. **AGF**	F	6			13.377,5	2,4
13. **BNP**	F		6		13.349,3	2,4
14. **BNL**	I		7		12.096,9	2,2
15. **Commerzbank**	D		8		11.392,8	2,0
16. **Bayerische Vereinsbank**	D		9		11.030,5	2,0
17. **San Paolo di Torino**	I		10		9.937,4	1,8
18. **Lloyds bank**	GB		11		9.380,5	1,7
19. **Münchener Rück**	D	7			9.077,9	1,6
20. **Aachener & Münchener**	D	8			8.737,9	1,6
Subtotal					349.856,2	62,9
Rest					205.924,8	37,1
Total					555.781,0	100,0

Three insurance conglomerates spread over the first three places: Allianz, AXA and UAP precede three credit conglomerates (Crédit Lyonnais, Deutsche Bank and Crédit Agricole) and a mixed financial conglomerate (the ING Group). Also remarkable in this top 20 is the great amount of German and French institutions.

The 36.714,8 mln ECU of Allianz is 6,6% of the total income of the 77 groups of which we have financial data. The French AXA group is the second largest insurance group, followed by the French insurer UAP. Normally, UAP is the second European insurer, but we considered more than only premium income in our analyses; this is probably the reason why AXA is larger than UAP.

Crédit Lyonnais is the biggest conglomerate if we look at the total income of credit conglomerates (24.732,0 mln. ECU), closely followed by Deutsche Bank and Crédit Agricole.

If we consider the mixed holdings the Dutch ING Group is the largest group. We have to admit that we only have found five groups, structured around a central holding company. The second group in this category is the Dutch/Belgian group

Fortis, a co-operation between the Belgian AG insurance group and the Dutch Amev/VSB group (a financial conglomerate on itself).

Table 3.7: Overview of the financial data: the biggest "conglomerates" by balance sheet total (1992).

3.7.a: Top 5: "Insurance conglomerates".

	Conglomerate	Country	Absolute figure (mln ECU)	%
1.	**Allianz**	D	105.466,4	15,1
2.	**GAN**	F	104.430,2	15,0
3.	**UAP**	F	102.488,9	14,7
4.	**AXA**	F	99.451,2	14,3
5.	**AGF**	F	51.565,7	7,4
	Subtotal		463.402,4	66,5
	Rest		233.568,6	33,5
	Total		696.971,0	100,0

3.7.b: Top 5: "Credit conglomerates".

	Conglomerate	Country	Absolute figure (mln ECU)	%
1.	**Crédit Lyonnais**	F	285.245,1	7,0
2.	**Deutsche Bank**	D	253.579,7	6,3
3.	**Crédit Agricole**	F	241.152,8	6,0
4.	**BNP**	F	235.126,0	5,8
5.	**ABN-AMRO Holding**	NL	207.952,5	5,1
	Subtotal		1.223.056,1	30,2
	Rest		2.828.199,2	69,8
	Total		4.051.255,3	100,0

3.7.c: Top 3: Mixed holdings.

	Conglomerate	Country	Absolute figure (mln ECU)	%
1.	**ING**	NL	105.147,9	47,0
2.	**ASLK Holding**	B	57.746,6	25,8
3.	**Fortis**	NL/B	38.586,4	17,2
	Rest	B	22.288,3	10,0
	Total		223.769,3	100,0

Again, Allianz, Crédit Lyonnais and ING are the biggest conglomerates. Compare the differences between the figures of the credit institutions with the figures of the insurance and mixed conglomerates. In the top-15, there are 13 credit institutions, which is of course normal in view of their business activities.

Therefore, it is dangerous to compare conglomerates on the basis of the total balance sheets. This is a very important conclusion in the discussion whether a conglomerate has a rather insurance or a "bank" character. One of the possible criterions was the balance sheet total. The figures in the tables have shown that one could make wrong conclusions if you just consider balance sheet total. Therefore, we argue that other criteria should also be taken into account if this decision is to be made.

Table 3.8: Overview of the financial data: the biggest "conglomerates" by number of employees (1992).

	Conglomerate	Country	Insurance conglom.	Credit conglom.	Mixed holding	Absolute figure	%
1.	Barclays Bank	GB		1		105.000	6,7
2.	NatWest	GB		2		95.200	6,1
3.	Allianz	D	1			74.504	4,8
4.	Deutsche Bank	D		3		74.256	4,8
5.	Credit Agricole	F		4		73.750	4,7
6.	Credit Lyonnais	F		5		71.446	4,6
7.	Lloyds Bank	GB		6		63.715	4,1
8.	BNP	F		7		56.354	3,6
9.	ING	NL			1	51.010	3,3
10.	ABN AMRO Holding	NL		8		47.854	3,1
11.	Midland Bank	GB		9		46.008	3,0
12.	Dresdner Bank	D		10		45.834	2,9
13.	Société Générale	F		11		45.158	2,9
14.	AXA	F	2			43.340	2,8
15.	Banco Central Hispano Americano	E		12		39.352	2,5
16.	Rabobank	NL		13		39.280	2,5
17.	TSB	GB		14		36.878	2,4
18.	Generali	I	3			33.311	2,1
19.	Crédit Mutuel	F		15		30.000	1,9
20.	BBV	E		16		29.267	1,9
	Subtotal					1.101.517	70,8
	Unknown					16	
	Rest					454.759	29,2
	Total					1.556.276	100,0

The list of companies, ranked by total number of employees is headed by Barclays Bank and National Westminster, two credit institutions of the UK. This is quite remarkable because these institutions were not mentioned in the previous tables.

In general, we find more British (credit) institutions in comparison with former tables.

The position of Allianz is also remarkable if you take into consideration that the second largest insurer with respect to this criterion (AXA) is ranked at number 14 and Generali is to be found at number 18.

The great number of credit institutions in the list can be explained by the fact that the intermediaries of banks are picked up in the payroll while insurers often work with independent intermediaries.

As one can deduct from the lists, the financial conglomerate movement is not a marginal phenomenon. The companies mentioned in the lists belong to the biggest of their respective countries.

We also made other computations to show the importance of this movement. First, we tried to catch the premium income of all financial conglomerates in the database and we have compared this figure with the total premium income of the EU (this amounts 321,74 mrd. ECU). We had only figures of 40 of them: these 40 conglomerates together had a premium income which represents 44% of the EU total[8].

We think the first effect is more important than the second one. Consequently, we think that the total premium income amounts to more than the 44 % of the EU total which we have found. However, we can't support these suppositions with clear and obvious figures.

In the following tables, we give aggregate figures for the different countries of the EU (table 3.9) and for the different types of financial conglomerates (table 3.10).

Table 3.9 shows - for each country - the number of conglomerates found, the aggregate number of employees, the aggregate balance sheet total and the total income of those congomerates.

---

[8]   This figure has to be corrected in two directions.
- We had figures of the premium income of 40 financial conglomerates; of course there are more financial conglomerates with insurance activities in the EU. The figures of these companies should also be taken into account if we are calculating the relative importance of the conglomeration movement. This means an upgrade of the present figure.
- On the other hand, some financial conglomerates have insurance activities outside the EU. The total premium income included these figures. This means that we made an obvious overestimation of the total premium income of the 40 financial conglomerates of which we had figures.

Table 3.9: Overview of the financial data by country (1992).

Country	Number	Employees	Bal. sh. total (mln. ECU)	Total income (mln. ECU)
Belgium	11	56.152	365.029,4	32.273,5
Denmark	4	7.709	23.544,9	4.499,8
France	14	374.501	**1.654.988,7**	**191.951,5**
Germany	8	265.872	827.680,7	116.180,3
Great Britain	11	**420.693**	735.350,3	53.359,1
Ireland	2	27.524	45.614,3	3.966,9
Italy	8	118.641	540.944,1	70.822,5
Luxembourg	1	?	5.313,5	466,8
The Netherlands	12	164.471	516.750,6	51.372,8
Portugal	1	3.998	8.681,2	1.238,5
Spain	5	116.715	248.097,7	29.649,5
Total	77	1.556.276	4.971.995,4	555.781,2

From this table, we can see that the aggregate balance sheet total and the aggregate total income are the greatest in France. This isn't remarkable at all: in France we found 14 groups.

Of course, these figures as shown in this table are only significant if they can be compared with aggregate figures of the countries' employees total, balance sheet total and total income. It's a pity that we couldn't obtain these aggregate figures.

The same can be said of the figures shown in table 3.10. Anyhow, we have showed them to give an overview of the distribution between the different types of enterprises.

Table 3.10: Overview of the financial data by the kind of enterprise of the active company (1992).

Country	Number	Employee	Bal. sh. total (mln. ECU)	Total income (mln. ECU)
Credit institution	47	1.239.476 (79,6)	4.051.255,1 (81,5)	329.708,4 (59,3)
Insurance institution	25	255.212 (16,4)	696.971 (14,0)	189.535,2 (34,1)
Mixed holding	5	61.588 (4,0)	223.769,3 (4,5)	36.537,6 (6,6)
Total	77	1.556.276 (100)	4.971.995,4 (100)	555.781,2 (100)

In our "sample", there were more credit institutions than insurance institutions (and mixed holdings): 47 credit institutions vs. 25 insurance institutions and 5 mixed holdings.

The credit institutions contribute by far more to the total number of employees and the aggregate balance sheet total. This can partly be explained by specific characteristics of their business activities:

- as already mentioned, most banks distribute their products with own employees, while an important part of the insurance products are distributed through independent agents and brokers;
- the balance sheet total of banks in comparatively more "voluminous" than the one of insurance companies, because it contains all monetary transactions with clients as well as in relation to inter-bank funding; the off-balance sheet evolution is certainly decreasing this difference.

4. Financial conglomerates; Risks?

L.A.A. Van den Berghe
Erasmus Finance & Insurance Centre (NL)
De Vlerick School voor Management (B)

4.1. WHAT ARE THE POTENTIAL RISKS IN RELATION TO FINANCIAL CONGLOMERATES ?

The economic literature, but above all the supervisory authorities point to a number of dangers and risks connected to the operation of financial conglomerates. What are their main concerns ?

4.1.1. THE RISKS OF INSTABILITY AND INSOLVENCY

The supervisory authorities are especially afraid of the following risks:

- *The risk of double gearing*:
  in the optimisation of their funding, holdings can be inclined to use their funds several times, that is, for both the parent company and the subsidiairies. This could mean that their "net" or "consolidated" solvency is much lower than the sum of the own funds of the members of the conglomerate. Cross shareholdings and other kinds of investments in daughter- or sister-companies are forms which lead to double gearing especially in cases where there is no consolidated approach.
  This kind of risk attracted a lot of attention in recent discussions in Europe. Especially banking supervisors are concerned about the possibility of banks participating in insurance companies. Their own funds may then serve twice as guarantee-capital (both for their banking activities as well as for their insurance activities).

- *increasing the total business risk*:
  this can be the case if the respective business risks are not offsetting one another but on the contrary if risks are of an incremental nature (e.g. lending to

a company in which the lender already participates, insuring the credit risks of a banking sister, etc.). The BCCI scandal has alarmed the supervisory authorities of the danger of excessive risk concentration resulting from intra-group transactions.

- *risk of contagion*:
  this relates to the risk that problems and certainly insolvency of one member of the group will deteriorate the position of all other members.The risk of contagion is also referred to as the risk of large financial exposures[1]. A risk of contagion could occur in case of participations or loans between members of the conglomerate, or if one member just contributes to another member in case of problems[2]. Even in the case of strict legal separation there could exist the danger of contagion in case that image and market-approach of the financial conglomerate as one entity is harmed by the financial distress of one member[3].

In an official speech, the director general of the Financial Services Directorate of the European Commission (Mogg - 1993) stated that supervisors are unanimous that double gearing of capital should be prevented in any group (insurance, banking or financial conglomerate). Nevertheless there is a divergence of view on how to cope with this double gearing and with the monitoring of financial risks in general.

According to recent research by Hesberg & Karten (1993) these dangers may however not be overestimated. They conclude that only in the case of "considerable positively correlated risk"[4] or with a "high rate of reciprocal shareholding" it may be justified to reduce balance sheet equity for solvency control. Aside from the "puffing effect" of cross-shareholdings, there is also a risk-spreading effect of the resulting diversified participations that increases the solvency of the total. Moreover they state that shares in (other) financial institutions should not be treated differently from e.g. shares in a brewery or a cotton mill.

---

[1]   See C.E.A. (1993) pp. 12-13.
[2]   This can be demonstrated by the way American Express communicated their financial help to their insurance branch: "ownership has its obligations".
[3]   An example is the experience of General Accident with their branch bank in New-Sealand (NZI Bank); the big losses had to be made up by the mother-company.
[4]   They conclude that :
      - a complete reduction of the equity capital by shares should only be considered in the totally unrealistic case of a complete dependence or correlation of all risks;
      - a partial reduction of the free assets by the (partial) value of the shares is justified if and only if a reciprocal interrelation or any other feed-back exists or if positively correlated risks threaten the companies in the group.
      They state that in general the parallellisms seem to be less frequent than the supervisory authority is afraid of.

4.1.2. THE RISK OF NON-TRANSPARENCY

Complex relations within a holding and between the members of the group create the fear that the supervision will be hampered to a considerable extent. Supervisors mainly point at the following potential risks:

- *the risk of regulatory arbitrage*:
  as any rational economic being, a financial conglomerate can be inclined to search for the most efficient way in establishing the legal structures, the head office, etc.; as long as important differences will prevail in the supervisory systems, companies can be tempted to look for the way of the least resistance; this can lead to circumventing the necessary rules, a risk which supervisors want to eliminate;
- *the risk of the metamorphose effect*:
  equity of subsidiaries (in the first, second, third degree etc.) can be financed by loans from the mother company. Through complex financial relations it can be very difficult for lenders to detect the final use of the funds of the parent company and for supervisors of the subsidiaries to detect the financial source of the funds;
- *the risk of opaque structures*:
  the larger the conglomerates, the more enterprises involved and the more complex their relationships, the more difficult it becomes for supervisors to have a clear view on the right cost calculations, on the localisation of business risks and on the lines of control. In these cases it will be harder for the supervisor to prove dumping or cannibalising of products[5].
  Some[6] hold the opinion that non-transparancy could also lead to a bigger chance of fraudulent actions.

4.1.3. THE RISK OF INFRINGING THE FREE COMPETITION AND THE RIGHTS OF THE CONSUMER

Different potential risks that could hamper the optimal market operations and/or the protection of the customer can be mentioned:

- *the risk of decreasing competition and abuse of power*:
  the more concentrated a market is, the more the free competition can be hampered; the fear of a great number of supervisors of banks and insurance companies goes further beyond this market risk in pointing to the danger of

---

[5] An example was given by an EC-official (Pearson, P. -1992, p. 11): "Much of the exponential growth in sales of life assurance via banks is at the very expense of the banks' own retail deposits. This makes it difficult to assess banks' profitability in relation to other group members".

[6] The Dutch Central Bank seems to take that view (see de Swaan - 1992).

"abuse of power" through interlocking directorship, mutual forbearance and concentration of power.

However there are some counter-arguments. On the basis of research in the U.S.A. and Canada, the Canadian Bankers Association[7] stated that: "..., the argument that the integration of financial services will result in excessive concentration of power in the hands of big banks is supported neither in theory nor by fact".

In this respect one may not neglect the fact that concentration -as a relative concept- is not only influenced by the number of players, but also by the market volume and the type of players. The enlargement of the market to the Common Market and even to the "global village" is decreasing the concentration. The same can be said from the perspective of the all finance revolution and the blurring of the boundaries between banks, saving institutions, insurance companies, investment firms etc. Through this blurring of the boundaries, the number of suppliers has been multiplied to a large extent;

- *the risk of conflicts of interest*:

  such conflicts can exist if a supplier has the choice between two or more options, and this choice is not neutral for himself nor for his enterprise. In this case the interests of the client and of the supplier can be opposite.

  Another example of conflicts of interest can be found in the potential opposition between the best choice for one client and the repercussions of this on another one.

  Research of the European Commission revealed that the risk of conflicts of interest increases with the number of activities or products offered[8]. Nevertheless we want to stress that the risk of conflicts of interest is not only relevant for financial conglomerates, but does exist in all types of enterprises that offer substitutable products or services.

4.2. THE SUPERVISION OF FINANCIAL CONGLOMERATES

The supervision of financial conglomerates is a heavy debated subject for the moment. As long as an agreement on the international level has not been reached, any detailed analysis can be outdated rather soon. Therefore we will limit the overview to the most important aspects under discussion.

Before entering into this analysis we want to stress the fact that most national supervisory systems as well as the European ones were all structured in view of the traditional boundaries between banks, insurance companies and investment firms (the so-called vertical division of activities). The market evolution in the direction of financial conglomerates, all finance, package solutions, integrated product

---

[7]   Maycock, J. (1986).

[8]   See also R.M.Goode (1986).

development etc. leads to the blurring of the traditional boundaries (the so-called horizontal integration and product clustering). This raises the question whether the actual legal solutions and structures are still adapted to the new wave in the financial sector.

Due to the fact that the European (and most of the national) supervisory authorities established different directives for banks, insurance companies and investment services, the phenomenon of "integrated" financial services and of financial conglomerates has until recently not been recognised as a separate topic.

One of the leading examples on a national level is found in the Netherlands. The first "Protocol" between the bank and the insurance supervisor to organise the supervision on integrated financial groups dates back to 1990. Recently an actualised and more detailed collaboration Protocol has been established[9].
The first official step on an international level in the direction of co-ordinating on the supervision of those three "sectors" was taken by the EC, in the so-called BCCI-directive[10]. The most relevant elements of this directive are the following:
- the structure of a financial group must be transparent; opaque structures and relationships are forbidden; supervisors have the right to refuse or revoke licences if they feel that the structure of a group is too opaque to allow effective supervision; detailed information must be forwarded to the respective supervisory authorities at the start of a concern as well as at any point in time when important changes take place;
- major shareholders and managers of financial conglomerates have to be "suitable" persons; therefore the supervisors have the authority to apply "fit and proper" criteria and eventually oppose against certain "non-qualifying" persons; since financial conglomerates are not directly under supervision, the EC warns that these measures have to be applied in a flexible way (Mogg - 1993);
- the head office of a financial institution must be located in the country of registration and this with the view of circumventing the risk of arbitrage;
- detailed guidelines are prescribed for the exchange of information between the different types of supervisory authorities and the external accountants have strict tasks in signalising potential problems to the relevant authorities.

The regulation of financial conglomerates themselves is under preparation. The most important questions under study are the following:

- *rules in relation to the formation of financial conglomerates*:
  When asking the question "who owns who?", a distinction must be made between:

---

9   Protocol (1994).
10   COM (93) - 363 - 28.7.1993.

- "downstream" or asset-restrictions: In what kind of enterprises can a bank or an insurance company participate/invest?
- "upstream" or liability-restrictions: Who is allowed to be the owner of a bank or an insurance company?

- *rules in relation to major shareholders and executives of a financial conglomerate*:

    As mentioned, according to the EC-directives major shareholders and managers of financial conglomerates must satisfy certain criteria of fitness and properness. Although these rules do not apply for holding-companies, the European Commission recently stated that supervisors could oppose against "non-qualifying" shareholders or executives[11]. There has been suggested that every[12] subsidiairy should have an independent board of directors for which even standards concerning good reputation and experience should play a role.

- *rules in relation to the accepted range of activities*:

    These rules could relate to the question which activities are allowed on an "own account basis" but also to the question which activities are accepted on an "agency" basis. Examples are: to what extent are banks allowed to cover risks, is engagement of banks and insurance companies in share-trading allowed and may they sell participations in investment funds? The prohibition for banks to cover risks and for insurance companies to take money on deposit isn't disputed according to the European Commission[13]. There are no EC-restrictions regarding co-operation of banks and insurance companies in the field of distribution.

- *rules in relation to the transparancy of the structure of a financial conglomerate*:

    According to the European Commission[14] supervisors must have the authority to withhold or withdraw entrance in case of a non-transparant structure of shareholders or management.

- *rules in relation to consolidation of financial conglomerates*:

    Consolidation is often suggested in order to increase transparancy and to get a better insight in both the totality as well as the components. However when discussing the obligation to consolidate, a distinction must be made between consolidation as a reporting technique and consolidation as a supervisory instrument.

    It seems that complete consolidation (especially in accounting terms) will not

---

[11]   Clarotti, P. (1992) stated this as follows: "It is clear that we cannot claim, that what we have achieved or about to put into place.....will give the right solution for the problems emerging from the proliferation of financial conglomerates".

[12]   It is questionable if this holds for all types of subsidiaries, financial as well as non-financial subsidiaries.

[13]   Fitchew, G.E. (1992) p. 9.

[14]   Clarotti, P. (1992) p. 9.

be feasible in the near future. Obstacles could be that there are various systems governing valuation and reporting and different definitions of the components that may constitute available solvency.
- *rules in relation to accounting controls*:
  Several motions are brought up for discussion in the field of accounting controls.
- *rules in relation to the protection of information files*:
  This relates to the exchange of databases and information about customers between different enterprises of the conglomerate (privacy protection becomes an important issue, especially in an information age).
- *rules in relation to cross-selling and conditional sales*:
  Topics for discussion in this respect are e.g. rules in relation to information about the final responsibility and the status of the distributor/producer; but also rules in relation to the linking of products, especially from the perspective of the obligation to buy "couples" of products (e.g. in packages, combined complementary products such as a mortgage, a life insurance and a fire insurance).
- *rules in relation to the prevention of double gearing*[15]:
  Different solutions are under discussion, such as complete consolidation (as is the case for the banking sector), partial consolidation (of the solvency fund), the deduction method (elimination of intra-group loans and participations), etc..
  Most banking supervisors opt for a supervision of the financial conglomerates on a consolidated basis (as is already the case for the banking sector). According to the European Commission (Mogg - 1993) this implies that the financial position of all banks and non-banks-financial institutions is consolidated (netting out all intra-group participations) and that one single minimum solvency is required.
  In our opinion, a complete consolidation is not realistic for the moment, not in the least because of the following differences between banking and insurance:
  - the calculation of the necessary solvency capital and the determination of the "free assets" differ to a considerable extent (see also chapter 5);
  - in the banking business the balance sheet is the main reference point for estimating the "core business", while for insurance it is especially the technical part of the profit and loss account that measures the "underwriting activity"; in Europe the GAAP-measures are not followed for life insurance, so that even the "saving products" that resemble to a large extent to banking products are all booked as turnover, while the parallel banking product is not integrated in the profit and loss account; only the "net"

---

[15] An inventory of national rules and techniques to prevent the multiple use of own funds can be found in C.E.A. (1993) pp 10-11.

intermediation margin is integrated as banking income[16].

We would therefore suggest that the solo-plus supervisory approach is a far better solution for the moment (see next point);

- *rules in relation to the responsibility for the supervision of financial conglomerates*:

Different options are feasible: a new type of supervisory authority, a joint or college solution, the solo-plus system, etc. Especially the last approach, developed in the Netherlands[17] has a good change to arrive at a consensus. It means that every supervisory authority sticks to his own business sector and supervisory rules and adds to this some extra measures to control the relations with and within the concern or holding. Although insurance groups would also be controlled on a group basis (extension of the home country control principle), no full consolidation of the solvency requirements and asset reglementations - even within the insurance sector - would be obliged.

- *rules in relation to the establishment of "Chinese walls" in order to prevent potential conflicts of interest*:

Chinese walls can best be defined as follows: "A Chinese Wall means an established arrangement whereby information known to persons in one part of a business is not available (directly or indirectly) to those involved in another part of the business and it is accepted that in each of the parts of the business so divided decisions will be taken without reference to any interest which any other such part or person in any such part of the business may have in the matter"[18]. Also "ethical codes" as well as "free competition" can decrease the danger that the interests of the clients are not the prime driver in the production of financial services.

---

[16] For more details see Ernst & Young (1993).
[17] For more details see Verzekeringskamer (1992) "Supervision of conglomerates, Advantages and disadvantages of 'consolidated' and 'solo-plus' supervision" and Verzekeringskamer (1993) "An analyses of "solo-plus" supervision".
[18] Maycock, J. (1986) p.79.

5. Solvency regulations for financial conglomerates

L.A.A. Van den Berghe
J. Roos
Erasmus Finance & Insurance Centre (NL)
De Vlerick School voor Management (B)

For the moment there is no specific regulation for financial conglomerates and consequently no specific requirements exist in relation to their solvency. We therefore paid special attention to the comparison of the solvency regulations for banks and insurance companies. We have tried to compare both aspects of the solvency regulations:

- the methods to calculate the required level of solvency;
- the definitions of the components that constitute the solvency fund.

The large differences between the approach used for the credit institutions[1] versus the one used for the insurance companies, make it necessary to look more thoroughly at the philosophy behind these differences.

In our opinion, this research is more than relevant since a number of changes or innovations are uttered in this respect:

- shouldn't the solvency requirements of banks and insurance groups be more in line with each other?
- shouldn't the solvency norm for insurance firms be amended to integrate also the investment risks and to what extent is an "actualisation" of the minimum solvency requirements necessary?
- shouldn't the risks of using derivatives and other off-balance sheet activities by insurers be monitored more carefully?
- shouldn't financial conglomerates use a more integrated approach towards the calculation of solvency and is such a global approach feasible?

---

[1] It is essential that attention is also paid to the rules for investment firms. This new regulation which must be applied before January 1, 1996 is however not included in this book.

We combined this qualitative research with a quantitative analysis. The qualitative research is integrated in this chapter, while the statistical analysis is summarised in chapter 6. Simulations of the potential impact of changes in the calculation methods will also be presented in that chapter.

5.1.   CALCULATION OF THE REQUIRED LEVEL OF SOLVENCY FOR CREDIT INSTITUTIONS AND FOR INSURANCE COMPANIES

5.1.1. CREDIT INSTITUTIONS

Appendix 5.A. gives a detailed overview of the previous and actual calculation methods of the minimum level of the solvency fund for credit institutions as prescribed by the European Commission. We will not analyse these prescriptions in detail, but only highlight the main aspects.

The determination of the required solvency level of banks has been broadened from a capital-to-assets ratio to a risk-assets ratio.

According to the capital-to-assets ratio the required level of the solvency fund is proportional to the volume of assets.

Important evolutions in the international banking activity necessitated the introduction of a new "risk assets" ratio:

-   the problems with the Third World debt-crisis alarmed the international financial sectors. Through the increasing debt risks, supervisors realised that it was necessary to differentiate the assets of a credit institution according to the degree of risks involved.
    Two types of indicators are used to measure the credit risk of the "assets": the type of creditor and the country of the creditor. The creditors are divided into different categories[2] (leading to four levels of risk which require respectively 0, 20, 50 or 100% of solvency capital); the countries are classified into 2 categories (zone A with roughly the OECD-countries and zone B with all other countries);
-   the introduction of all types of off-balance sheet transactions (securitisation, derivatives) increased the risks run by credit institutions. This development was (partly) a method to circumvent the solvency requirements, previously based on the "balance sheet"-total.
    Here the credit risk is not only measured on the basis of the former two elements (type of creditor and country of the creditor) but also on the basis of a

---

[2]   For more details see appendix 5.A.

third element, the "credit conversion degree". Besides this credit risk, the important interest rate risks and exchange risks must eventually be taken into account. The introduction of the new rules on investment activities will also lead to the integration of other market risks[3];

- it has been decided recently that also "large exposures" must lead to higher solvency requirements.
  Large risks are defined as loans which are greater than 10% of the own funds of the credit institutions. Two measures are taken to limit the exposure of those loans:
  * such large loans are considered as high risks, so that they require a 100% of the solvency capital[4];
  * the exposure is restricted on an individual basis (may not be greater than 20 or 25% of the own funds) as well as on a global basis (the total amount of outstanding large loans may not be greater than 8 times the own funds).

The risk assets ratio is differentiating the required solvency margin according to the degree of risks involved. This means that assets that can be considered as rather risky do need extra solvency margins to be held, while nearly riskless assets do not affect the level of the required solvency margin.

The solvency margin required is thus related to the volume of business. This proportional solvency rule is completed with an absolute minimum level (especially relevant for starting institutions and smaller enterprises). The minimum norm for credit institutions is 5 million ECU; only in exceptional cases a lower minimum (1 to 5 million ECU) will be accepted.

5.1.2. INSURANCE COMPANIES

The detailed analysis of the calculation methods used to define the solvency requirements for insurance companies is given in appendix 5.B. We will again limit this introduction to the main characteristics of these calculation methods. The most important aspects are the following:

- the solvency margin required is completely different for life and non-life companies;
- for the life companies the reference base is partly the liabilities (technical provisions) and partly the insurance risk (capital under risk);
  for the liability risk a distinction is made according to the term of the contract and the degree of investment risk carried by the insurer:
  * short(er) term contracts carry less underwriting risk, so that the solvency

---

[3]   See appendix 5.B.
[4]   Exceptions are possible (0 or 20%) : for more details see appendix 5.A.

needs are lower: 0,1% or 0,15% of the capital under risk instead of 0,3%;

* contracts, which do not guarantee a fixed return, transfer the investment risk to the insured (e.g. unit linked insurance); consequently the level of solvency needed is much lower (1% instead of 4% of the mathematical reserves)[5];

- for the non-life companies no balance sheet elements at all are taken into account; the reference base differs according to the profitability of the business; if an insurance company sets her tariffs too low (and has a technical cost ratio of more than ±70% of her premium income) the indicator will be the "average claims due"[6]; on the contrary if the tarification is set at sufficient profitable levels, then the premiums will be the reference base on which the solvency requirements will be based[7];

- the solvency requirements can be decreased through the use of reinsurance; for non-life business a maximum decrease up to 50% of the necessary level is possible; for the life risks a distinction is made between the liability risk (with a potential decreasing effect through reinsurance up to 15%) and the underwriting risk (with the same rule as for the non-life risks, i.e. 50% maximum decrease);

- the minimum level of the solvency fund is different according to the line of business. For the life insurance companies the minimum is set at 800.000 ECU. Exceptions are possible (e.g. for mutuals), so that this minimum is decreased to a level between 100.000 and 600.000 ECU.

For the non-life business, specialised companies should have the minimum level needed for their specialty branch. Companies with a mixed portfolio of non-life businesses must have the largest of the "relevant" minima. The levels vary between 200.000 and 400.000 ECU (but lower levels can be allowed for mutuals). Only for specialised credit insurance the minimum is much higher (1.400.000 ECU).

These minimum requirements are set to a lower level (50%) for companies which are not incorporated in the EU, but they will have to make a deposit (of 50% of their minimum solvency level) to guarantee their commitments. Large differences exists between these rules and the rules for the banking sector (paragraph 5.1.1).

---

[5]   For more details in respect to the investment risk of life insurance companies see chapter 6.

[6]   The rule is that the average is calculated over the previous three years; only for insurance with a "longer cycle" (credit insurance, storm insurance) the reference base is the average claims due over the previous seven years.

[7]   According to the actual level of profitability of the insurance companies, most companies will have to calculate their solvency requirements on the basis of the claims due.

5.2. CALCULATION OF THE SOLVENCY FUND FOR CREDIT INSTITUTIONS AND INSURANCE COMPANIES

Once the required level of the solvency margin has been calculated, one must analyse whether the institution involved has enough "free" funds to cover these solvency requirements. This means that we have to look after what types of funds can be taken into account to represent the solvency needed, but also after the degree to which these funds can be integrated as "representative values".

Neither of these elements are defined in the same way for credit- and insurance institutions. Although the differences between the banking and the insurance sector decreased since the last EU-directives became into force[8], a separate analysis of the respective regulations is still necessary.

5.2.1. CREDIT INSTITUTIONS

The calculation of the solvency fund for credit institutions distinguishes two types of funds:

- the tier 1 solvency is composed of the capital, reserves and the general banking fund; in principle, these components are taken for their total value;
- the tier 2 solvency is composed of funds with a lower quality or funds which are less secure (e.g. subordinated loans, revaluation reserves, value adjustments); consequently these funds are not taken for their total value but only for 50 or 25% of their book value.

  Corrections are eventually needed e.g. for own shares hold, for intangible assets or for subordinated loans or participations[9] in other credit institutions; this last correction is intended to overcome the danger of the so-called double gearing[10].

5.2.2. INSURANCE COMPANIES[11]

From the analysis of appendix 5.B. it is clear that the definition of the "free funds" that can constitute the solvency fund has been adapted recently to include quite a number of new elements. Most of these elements are in fact copied from the

---

[8] Think for instance at the integration of "subordinated loans" in the calculation of solvency funds for the insurance sector.

[9] In principle transactions larger than 10% of the capital of the enterprise in question (for more details see appendix 5.A.).

[10] However, in the context of the discussion about financial conglomerates it might be opportune to outline that there are no time or quantity limits for participations of credit institutions in other financial institutions, but the weight of certain equity participations in the risk assets volume is 100% and the calculation of the capital elements within the groups is subject to certain corrections.

[11] Special definitions are given for mutual companies. For more details see appendix 5.B.

definition of solvency components for credit institutions, such as subordinated loans and cumulative preferential share capital. These new regulations bring the definitions of solvency for both sectors more in line with each other. There remain however some important differences; we will only stress the main interesting differences.

As was the case with the calculation of the required level of the solvency margin, also the components that can constitute the solvency fund differ between life and non-life insurance companies.

For non-life companies the solvency is composed of the capital and reserves for their full value. For non-paid up capital, cumulative preferential share capital, subordinated loans, etc. only part of the book value is taken as "free funds". Although these last two components are new in the definition of the solvency fund, it is clear that the new definition is potentially more severe, because elements of "over-estimation" of liabilities and technical provisions are no longer accepted. To our opinion this is not completely justified, in as far as insurers face more and more difficult risks and can measure their "liabilities" less and less accurate (cfr. liability crises, problems of reinsurers, etc.).
Opposite to credit institutions, it is still allowed for non-life insurers to integrate "hidden reserves" and "under-estimation of assets" as solvency components.

Since life insurers face more upfront costs[12] and have "contractual" commitments over a much longer period of time, the calculation of their profitability and their solvency is more complicated than it is the case for non-life companies or for credit institutions. Therefore, besides the main solvency components, as defined for the non-life insurers, different types of hidden reserves and future profits can eventually be taken into account. The degree to which such extra solvency components can be integrated in the solvency calculations will differ according to the type of accounting system.
Quite diverging methods exist to account for the high up-front costs:

- At one extreme there is the very orthodox method of absorbing all up-front costs in the first year of the contract; this leads to net losses (on these contracts) in the first years and postponement of profits (and taxes) to later years. Consequently these companies have large hidden reserves, and these "implicit" funds can be taken into account for the calculation of the solvency fund.
- At the other extreme there are methods that are based on the appraisal value or the embedded value; the profits and reserves that are based on these calculation methods are much more in conformity with "economic" appreciation tech-

---

[12] Such as acquisition costs, contractual examinations, contract administration, etc.

niques in so far that the liabilities and the profitability accounted for are much more in line with realistic expectations. In principle, the resulting system doesn't allow for the existence of hidden reserves. Consequently the solvency calculation will not be based on implicit elements.

- In between there are methods as for example methods referred to as "Zillmerisation"[13.] Different "degrees" of Zillmerisation are possible, but they all have in common that the "liabilities" towards clients (mathematical reserve, surrender values) are corrected for the "up-front costs" which have not been repaid (completely) at that moment in time. This method however does not take into account the potential profitability of the written contracts and consequently this goodwill is a source of "hidden reserves". The "implicit funds" can be larger, if the Zillmerisation is only partially applied.

5.3. OTHER ELEMENTS THAT MUST GUARANTEE THE STABILITY AND CONFIDENCE IN THE FINANCIAL AND INSURANCE SECTOR

5.3.1. CREDIT INSTITUTIONS

Besides the solvency fund, the confidence in the financial system is also guaranteed through the existence of a deposit insurance system. Such a system creates a safety net for clients (saving, depositing their money) within certain limits and certain conditions, against the risk of failure of their credit institution.

Most industrial countries have a deposit insurance system but the institutional form and coverage differ markedly across countries. However, the EU has issued a directive, implying that all member states will have to adapt their deposit insurance schemes in such a way that certain minimum requirements are met (in Belgium the draft legislation is currently under review).

5.3.2. INSURANCE COMPANIES

The EU-rules do not require the insurance companies to set up a guarantee system or a "deposit insurance mechanism". This does not mean that clients of insurers can only rely on their solvency fund held by an insurer. On the contrary, quite a diverse set of instruments must guarantee the stability and reliability of the insurance sector:

---

[13] The "Zillmer-method" and other methods as the "Höckner-method" and the "release from risk method" are discussed from (among others) an accounting and an actuarial point of view in Oosenbrug (1993). See Oosenbrug (1994) for a short excerpt of this.

- the technical provisions form the first buffer; in the case of life insurance with an important saving element, these liabilities are the individual claims of the clients, comparable to any deposit or saving account of credit institutions; but for pure risk insurance these liabilities are the collective claim of the insured;
- for insured losses that have occurred, but for which the insurer has not yet received any concrete claim, an extra reserve is formed (the so-called IBNR reserve);
- for cyclical risks an extra reservation is made (egalisation reserve); this reservation has quite a great resemblance with the "general banking fund"; contrary to the credit institutions this fund is not considered as an element of the solvency fund of insurance companies, whereas for banks it is a component of the tier 1 funds;
- besides these "obligations to reserve" for liabilities, also numerous aspects of the investment of these reserves are regulated:
  * obligation to diversify the investments;
  * requirement of congruency and localisation of assets;
  * rules for the evaluation of these representative values.

5.4. PHILOSOPHY BEHIND THE SOLVENCY REQUIREMENTS FOR CREDIT INSTITUTIONS AND INSURANCE COMPANIES

We would like to point to the main differences in the regulation of credit institutions and insurance companies.

5.4.1. GENERAL OBSERVATIONS

Before going into the details of the solvency regulations, it is good to stress the differences in the main accents of the supervision of banks and insurance companies. For simplicity, we will limit this comparison to the EU-rules[14] and we will not enter into the details of the national applications of these EU-rules. This does not mean that these differences are of no importance, but our research focuses on the potential EU-regulation of financial conglomerates and not on national adaptations to these EU-directives. Moreover the national differences tend to decrease due to the home country control, the single licence and the harmonisation of supervisory approaches.

The analysis can best be divided according to the level aimed at:

- the philosophy behind the regulation at the micro-level is quite parallel for

---

[14] These rules are certainly the most relevant ones for the analysis of the insurance sector. For the banking sector also the international/global scenery is very relevant.

banks and insurance companies:

* the main aim of the supervision of both sectors is to protect the clients who own "financial assets" or "receivables" that are the "liability" of the banks or insurance companies. Especially the solvency regulations are prescribed to cover these needs for protection of the clients.

  In the case of credit institutions these liabilities relate to banking accounts, term deposits, saving accounts, etc. For life insurers it can be "contractual savings" and for all other types of insurance this relates to "non-individualised liabilities" of insurers against their policyholders and other parties concerned, whom they promised to refund eventual losses;

* some of the regulations (e.g. the accounting rules and the supervision of these accounts), are set up to lower the information gap, from which most of the mass clients suffer in valuing the reliability of the institutions in general, and their promises more specifically;

- the philosophy behind the regulation at the market-level is also quite parallel between banks and insurance companies:

- the third generation directives try to install the free competition, since that would be at the advantage of all clients: greater choice, innovation and better conditions;

- the philosophy behind the regulation at the macro-level is however quite different:

* the credit institutions are not only performing a function as "financial intermediary" but they are also crucial to the monetary system. Consequently the volume of their transactions and the remuneration of the different types of deposits and credits do influence the monetary system to a great extent, so the supervision of credit institutions is a fundamental instrument for the development of a monetary policy (e.g. interest rate structures, monetary mass, inflation rate, etc.).

  Here insurance companies only play a minor role, and are certainly not the leading institutions to develop the necessary monetary policy instruments;

* the regulation of the financial sector should procure the necessary macro-stability. In this respect there exists a greater parallel, but not a completely comparable situation between the banking and the insurance sector. Although "stability" and "thrust" are important ingredients of the "products" sold by both sectors, it is clear that these characteristics have more far reaching consequences in the banking sector. This again has to do with their "monetary" function; by transforming "banking accounts" into "credits" they influence the buying power, but this transformation process is built upon the premises of stability and thrust. Although the national banks can perform their function of "lender of the last resort", the financial payment system could become under great pressure when all clients ask simultaneously to cash their receivables (cfr. the liquidity crisis of the thirties). This is

certainly not comparable to the insurance business, where the largest amount of the "technical" liabilities is not "liquid". In fact, life insurance companies even transform a financial intermediation function in an opposite direction: they invest long term capital (even up to 40 years) into shorter term instruments (and consequently they suffer from a problem of matching assets with liabilities).

5.4.2. PHILOSOPHY BEHIND THE SOLVENCY REGULATIONS

The calculation of the required level of solvency as well as the definition of the components forming the solvency fund and the supplementary buffers to guarantee confidence in the financial system differ to a great extent between credit institutions and insurance companies:

- *Level of solvency*
  The calculation of the necessary level of solvency is based on the insights into the risks, from which the institutions under consideration can potentially suffer. Comparing the minimum solvency requirements, it must be observed that the banking risks need more solvency than the insurance risks; within the insurance sector the credit insurance is considered the most risky business, while the other non-life insurance branches consume less capital.
  For credit institutions no attention is given to potential liability risks; the only reference base is asset risks and "off-balance" risks. These risks are mainly credit risks, although also interest rate risks and exchange risks can be taken into account.
  These risks are measured on an institutional level; if a group structure exists, it will be the holding company that has to fulfill the solvency requirements. Insurance companies on the contrary, are less supervised on an institutional level; it is more the technical working level that is taken into account. This is logical in as far as the measures of the risks carried by insurers are mainly of a technical nature and differ according to the type of insurance branch. Moreover, the EC-directives oblige the insurance companies to specialise in either life, non-life, credit insurance etc.[15].
  Due to the inversion of the exploitation cycle the insurers' risks are first of all "liability risks". These are measured on the basis of certain liability components (for life insurers) but especially on the basis of underwriting risk indicators (premiums, claims, capital under risk). For non-life insurers even sanctions are foreseen if they do not use sufficient profitable tarification schemes. Asset risks are more supervised through specific prescriptions for investments and their valuation than through risk based solvency requirements. For life

---

[15]   Exceptions to this generalised specialisation requirement are possible for "existing" multi-branch companies.

insurers however there is an important solvency requirement in relation to the investment risks carried by the insurer: three quarters of the solvency requirements (based on the specific liabilities - mathematical reserves) can in fact be considered as a buffer against these investment risks[16].

For the moment no attention is paid to potential off-balance risks. This was certainly justified in the past, since not many insurers used these instruments. There is however an increasing tendency that (larger) insurance companies try to sophisticate their financial management and integration of certain off-balance instruments is becoming more and more popular.

- *Components of the solvency fund*
  The difference in the definition of the components, forming the solvency fund are decreased to a considerable degree since the third generation directives. Nevertheless there remains quite a substantial number of differences (see also appendix 5.C.):
  * integration of non paid-up capital for insurance companies;
  * integration of general banking fund (for credit institutions) and no integration of egalisation reserves (for insurers);
  * difference in the degree of integration of revaluation reserves (50% for banks and 100% for insurance companies) and value corrections (for banks);
  * difference in the degree of integration of subordinated loans and cumulative preferential shares;
  * integration of hidden reserves and future profits for life insurance companies;
  * under-estimation of assets for non-life insurance companies;
  * penalties for concentration of holdings of credit institutions in other credit institutions.

  In relation to this last factor, a discussion is going on whether the same rules should not be applied to insurance companies. It is not possible to go into detail on this important question. The only remark we want to make here is the following: although it is reasonable to overcome also double gearing in the insurance sector, it is clear that insurers as institutional investors can have considerable holdings in other companies and enterprises with pure investment perspectives. Therefore the distinction (analysed in chapter 1) between participations and investments is also important in this respect.

- *Extra buffers*
  The extra instruments that guarantee the solvency, stability and confidence in the financial sector are completely different. The banking sector is relying on

---

[16]   This is deducted from the comparison of the rules for life insurance with and without investment risk (respectively 4% and 1% of the mathematical reserve).

an extra deposit insurance that insures clients - within certain limits - against unfortunate or bad choices of their suppliers of financial services. The insurance sector is more relying on extra supervision and extra reservations. Another difference that should be mentioned is the fact that all banks are supervised while there is in principle no supervision of reinsurance companies (although there is an indirect control through the cession in reinsurance of the supervised direct insurers, but this does not relate to the so-called spiral effect of retrocessions).

Appendix 5.A.

Credit institutions

It is advisable to make a distinction between credit institutions and investment firms. The solvency rules for credit institutions are based on a risk assets ratio (EC Directive of 1989, which has now been implemented by all member states). For investment firms the requirements are outlined in the investment services and related capital adequacy Directive of 1993. For these firms the calculation of solvency requirements will be based on a ratio relating the market risks (general and specific risks, counterparty risk and exchange risk) to the so-called trading book. These rules require implementation before January 1, 1996. They will also apply to credit institutions, at least for the investment services they provide, next to the existing risk asset ratio requirements. The workshop did not include these new regulations on investment activities.

A.1. **WHAT IS THE MINIMUM LEVEL OF SOLVENCY?**

A.1.1. MINIMUM LEVEL OF SOLVENCY FROM 1-1-1993 UNTIL 1-1-1994

The solvency level is based on the solvency calculation and the minimum own funds of 5 mln. ECU.

-   Solvency calculation:

$$\frac{\text{Own Funds}}{\sum \text{weighted (assets and OBS elements)}} * 100\% \geq 8\% \quad (1)$$

A.1.2. KIND OF RISK

- Credit risk:

Table 1.1.: Indicators.

Type of creditor.	0%	20%	50%	100%
central governments/ central banks	* ab			* b
claims carrying the explicit guarantees of central governments and central banks	* ab			
European Union	*			
European Investment Bank (EIB)		*		
guaranteed by EIB		*		
Multilateral Development Bank (MDB)		*		
guaranteed by MDB		*		
regional and local government		* a		* b
guaranteed by regional and local governments		* a		
credit institutions		* ab		* b
guaranteed by credit institutions		* ab		
non-banking sector				*
secured to the satisfaction of the competent authorities ...	*	* eib/mdb	*	
cash in hand	*			
cash items in the process of collection		*		
prepayments and accrued income			*	
tangible assets				*
holdings of shares, participations and other components of the own funds of other credit institutions which are not deducted from the own funds of the lending institutions				*
all other assets				*

Type of country of the creditor
a = mostly members of the OECD
b = other countries

A.1.3. KIND OF RISK ONLY FOR OBS ACTIVITIES:

- Credit conversion degree:
  to what extent will the OBS activity result in an effective credit (= asset)?
- Interest risk (only for interest and exchange rate contracts)
- Exchange risk (only for interest and exchange rate contracts)

A.1.4. WEIGHTED ASSETS

Calculation:

$$\text{weighted assets} \ = \sum \left(\text{asset} * \text{weighting factor} \right) \ (2)$$

For a list of elements with the different kinds of weighting factors, see paragraph A.3.

A.1.5. WEIGHTED OFF-BALANCE-SHEET ELEMENTS

-   When only credit risk is taken into consideration.
    Calculation:

weighted OBS elements $= \sum \big($ OBS element $*$ weighting factor $*$ credit conversion factor $\big)$ (3)

OBS element with[17]	weighting factor
low risk	0%
medium\low risk	20%
medium risk	50%
high risk	100%

-   When interest and exchange risk are taken into consideration.
    There are two methods[18] for the calculation of the solvency requirements for interest and foreign-exchange contracts. The 'marking to market' approach and the 'original exposure' approach.
-   Exceptions:
    *   interest and exchange rate contracts on recognized exchanges;
    *   exchange rate contracts with an original maturity of 14 days or less.

There are no specific solvency requirements for these exceptions.

A.1.6. MINIMUM LEVEL OF SOLVENCY FROM 1-1-1994 UNTIL 1-7-95 (INCLUDING LARGE RISK)

-   Calculation of large risk:
    risk connected with a client or a group of united clients $\geq 10\%$ own funds (4)

-   Limitations:
    *   maximum 25% of own funds
    *   maximum 20% of own funds (if group company with a credit institutions)
    * $\sum$large risk ≤ 8 * own funds

-   Exceptions:
    *   can be given for "relative" smaller credit risk (weighting factor 0% or 20%);
    *   intra-group relations of consolidated firms.

---

[17]   See OJEC 89/647/EEC; annex 1.
[18]   See OJEC 89/647/EEC; annex 2.

- Solvency calculation:

$$\frac{\text{Own Funds}}{\sum \text{weighted (assets and OBS - elements)}_{NR} + \sum \text{(assets and OBS - elements)}_{LR}} * 100\% \geq 8\%$$

NR = normal risks   LR = large risks (5)

A.2. **COMPONENTS OF SOLVENCY**

- Own funds: 3 elements:
  * tier 1: core capital
  * tier 2: complementary components (lower quality of funds)
  * correction factors

Table 1.2: Own fund credit institutions from 1-1-1993[19].

	Own funds credit institutions	% SM.
1	paid up share capital	100%
	share premium accounts	100%
2	reserves	100%
	profits and losses brought forward	100%
3	revaluation reserves	50%
4	funds for general banking	100%
5	value adjustments of credit institutions' loans and advances, debt securities, shares and other variable-yield securities which are not held as financial fixed assets.	50%
6	* capital elements that fulfil certain conditions [20]	50%
	* securities of indeterminate duration and other instruments that fulfil the conditions required[21]	50%
	* cumulative preferential shares other than in point 8	50%
7	commitments of the members (co-operative societies)	25%
	commitments of the borrower (credit institution organized as funds)	25%
8	* fixed cumulative preferential shares	25%
	* subordinated loan capital (original maturity at least five years) (both under certain conditions[22])	25%
9	own shares at book value	-
10	intangible assets	-
11	material losses of the current financial year	-
12	* holdings in other credit and financial institutions ≥ 10% of their capital	-
	* subordinated loans and instruments mentioned in point 6 ≥ 10% own capital.	
13	a. holdings in other credit and financial institutions ≤ 10% their capital	-
	b. subordinated claims and instruments mentioned in point 6 (other than mentioned in point 12) ≥ 10% own capital.	
	(13a + 13b) - (10% of the sum of points 1-11)	

[19]   See OJEC 89/299/EEC.
[20]   See OJEC 89/299/EEC; article 3, point 1.
[21]   See OJEC 89/299/EEC, article 3, point 2.
[22]   See OJEC 89/299/EEC; article 4, point 3.

"-"   : correction factors
3 + 5 + 6 + 7 + 8   : complementary components
1 + 2 + 4   : core capital

- Requirements:
  3 + 5 + 6 + 7 + 8 ≤ 1 + 2 + 4 - 9 - 10 - 11
  7 + 8 ≤ 0,5 (1 + 2 + 4 - 9 - 10 - 11)

The total of items 12 and 13 shall be deducted from the total of all items.

A.3. RISK WEIGHTING FACTORS[23]

- Zero weighting
  * cash in hand and equivalent items;
  * asset items constituting claims on Zone A central governments and central banks;
  * asset items constituting claims on the European Communities;
  * asset items constituting claims carrying the explicit guarantees of Zone A central governments and central banks;
  * asset items constituting claims on Zone B central governments and central banks, denominated and funded in the national currencies of the borrowers;
  * asset items constituting claims carrying the explicit guarantees of Zone B central governments and central banks, denominated and funded in the national currency common to the guarantor and the borrower;
  * asset items secured, to the satisfaction of the competent authorities, by collateral in the form of Zone A central government or central bank securities, or securities issued by the European Communities, or by cash deposits placed with the lending institution or by certificates of deposit or similar instruments issued by and lodged with the latter;

- 20% weighting
  * asset items constituting claims on the European Investment Bank (EIB);
  * asset items constituting claims on multilateral development banks;
  * asset items constituting claims carrying the explicit guarantee of the European Investment Bank (EIB);
  * asset items constituting claims carrying the explicit guarantees of multilateral development banks;
  * asset items constituting claims on Zone A regional governments or local authorities;

[23] See OJEC 89/647/EEC article 6.

* asset items constituting claims carrying the explicit guarantees of Zone A regional governments or local authorities;
* asset items constituting claims on Zone A credit institutions but not constituting such institutions' own funds;
* asset items constituting claims, with a maturity of one year or less, on Zone B credit institutions, other than securities issued by such institutions which are recognized as components of their own funds;
* asset items carrying the explicit guarantees of Zone A credit institutions;
* asset items constituting claims with a maturity of one year or less, carrying the explicit guarantees of Zone B credit institutions;
* asset items secured to the satisfaction of the competent authorities, by collateral in the form of securities issued by the EIB or by multilateral development banks;
* cash items in the process of collection;

- 50 % weighting
  * loans fully and completely secured, to the satisfaction of the competent authorities, by mortgages on residential property which is or will be occupied or let by the borrower;
  * prepayments and accrued income: these assets will be subject to the weighting corresponding to the counterparty where a credit institution is able to determine it in accordance with Directive 86\635\EEC. Otherwise, where it is unable to determine the conterparty, it shall apply a flat-rate weighting of 50%;

- 100 % weighting
  * asset items constituting claims on Zone B central governments and central banks except where denominated and funded in the national currency of the borrower;
  * asset items constituting claims on Zone B regional governments or local authorities;
  * asset items constituting claims with a maturity of more than one year on Zone B credit institutions;
  * asset items constituting claims on the Zone A or Zone B non-bank sectors;
  * tangible assets
  * holdings of shares, participations and other components of the own funds of other credit institutions which are not deducted from the own funds of the lending institutions;
  * all other assets except where deducted from own funds.

Figure 1: capital requirements of credit institutions from 1-1-1993 to 1-1-94[24]

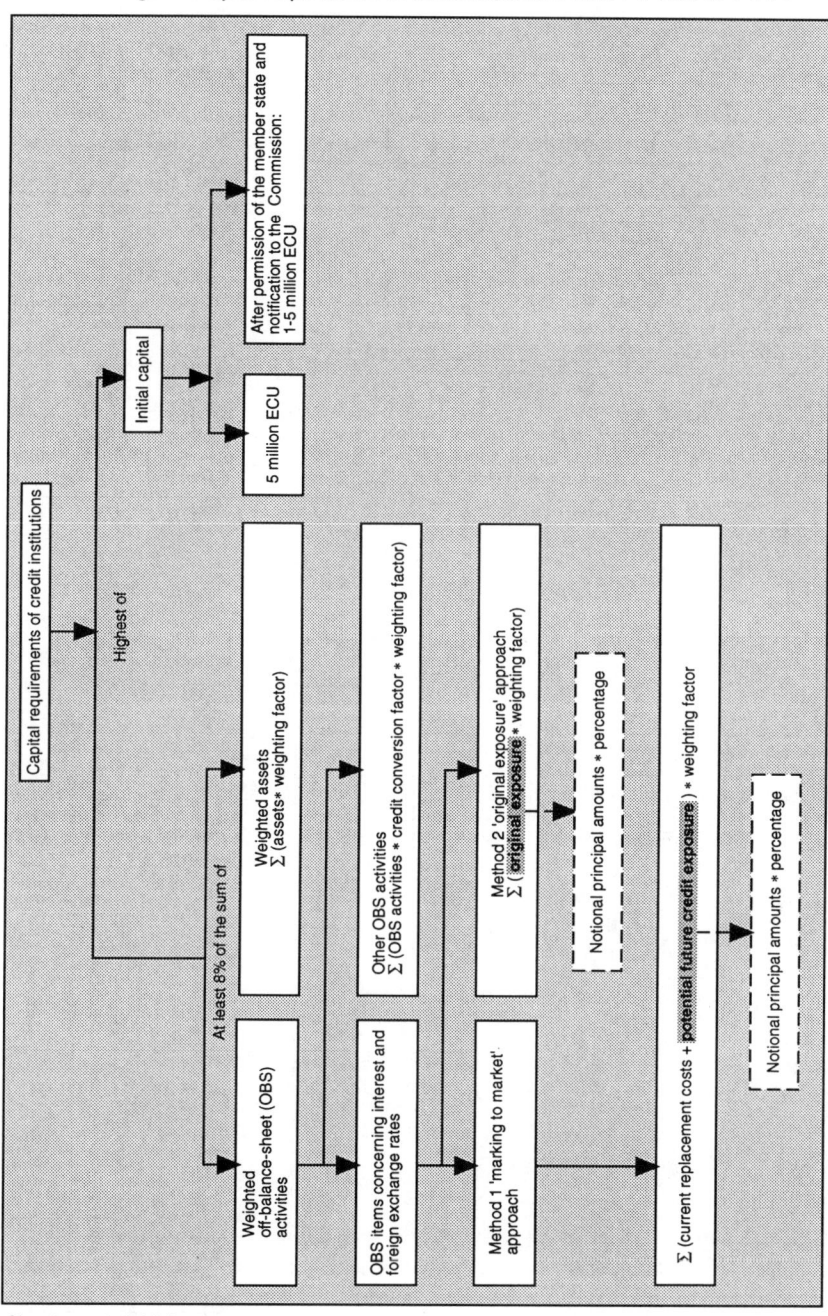

[24]   Roos, J. (1994)

Figure 2: capital requirements of credit institutions form 1-1-1994 to 1-7-1995[25].

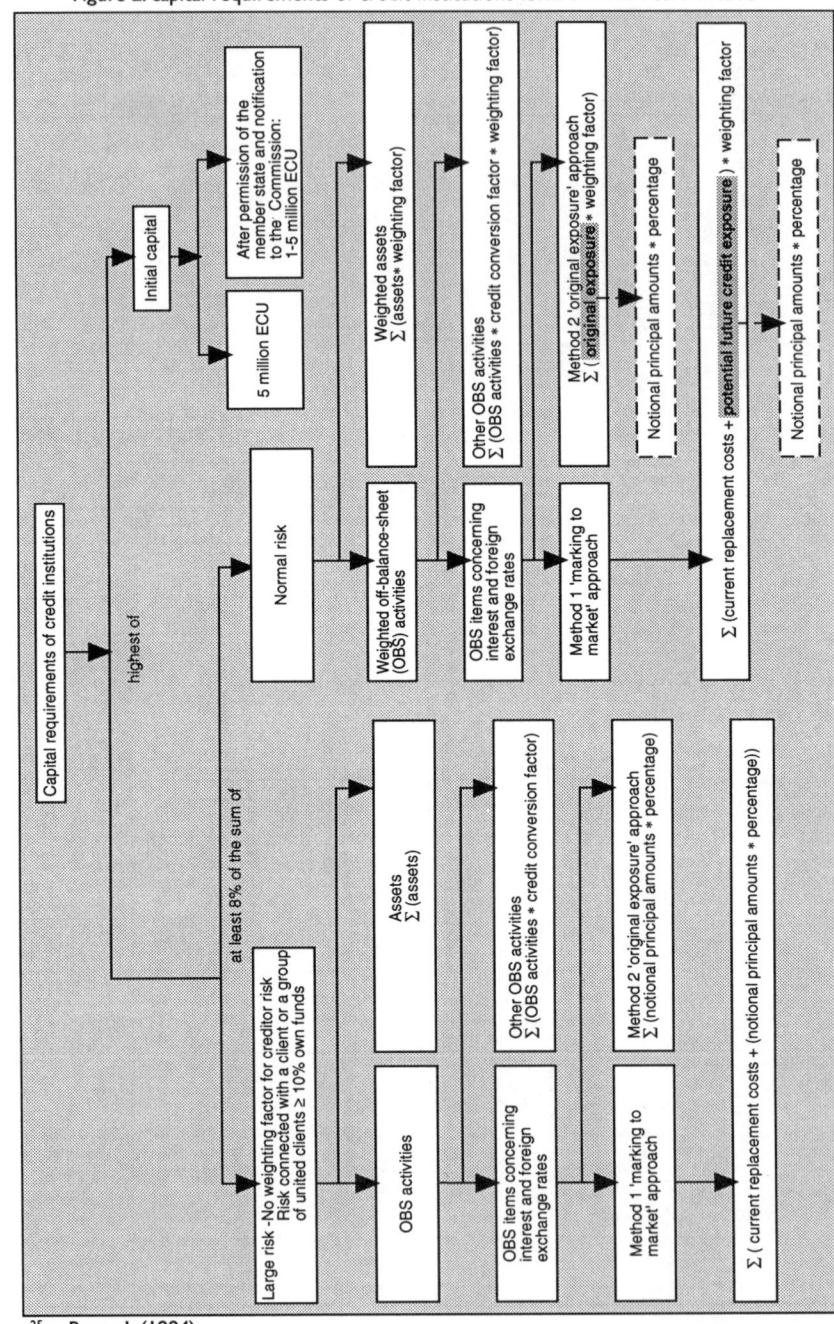

25   Roos, J. (1994)

Appendix 5.B.

Insurance companies

B.1. WHAT IS THE MINIMUM LEVEL OF SOLVENCY

B.1.1. NON-LIFE INSURANCE

The solvency level is based on the largest amount of:

- minimum guarantee fund;
- solvency margin based on premiums;
- solvency margin based on average claims.

Average claims are used as reference base unless
Claims/premiums < ±70%

B.1.2. MINIMUM GUARANTEE FUND

200.000, 300.000, 400.000 or 1.400.000 ECU depending on the kind of insurance branch.

B.1.3. SOLVENCY LEVEL BASED ON PREMIUMS ($X_{T.I}$)

- Components:
  - $+$ premiums or contributions due in respect of all direct business and all reinsurance;
  - total amount of premiums or contributions cancelled in the last financial year;
  - total amount of taxes;
  - total amount of levies pertaining to the premiums or contributions entering into the aggregate.

- Solvency calculation: (For the explanation of the symbols see paragraph B.3.)

* If premiums ≤ 10 mln. ECU:

$$SM = \left(X_{t-1}*18\%\right)*\frac{Sn}{Sb} \quad (1)$$

* If premiums > 10 mln. ECU:

$$SM = \left[\left(10\text{mln. ecu}*18\%\right)+\left(\left(X_{t-1}-10\text{mln. ecu}\right)*16\%\right)\right]*\frac{Sn}{Sb} \quad (2)$$

- Requirement:

$$\frac{Sn}{Sb} \geq 50\% \quad (3)$$

- Exceptions:
  * health insurance practised on a similar technical basis to that of life insurance.
    requirements: see OJEC (73/239/EEC) article 16, point 4.
    solvency calculation: formula (1) * 1/3
                                   formula (2) * 1/3

  * Lloyds: net premiums * flat rate percentage

This percentage is based on statistical data of commissions paid.

B.1.4. SOLVENCY LEVEL BASED ON AVERAGE CLAIMS (Z_{T-1})

- Claim components (Y_{t-1}):
  + claims paid in respect of direct business and reinsurance for the past three financial years (= reference period);
  + amount of provisions or reserves for outstanding claims established at the end of the reference period;
  - amount of claims paid during the reference period;
  - amount of provisions or reserves for outstanding claims established at the beginning of the reference period .

- Average claims: $Z_{t-1} = Y_{t-1}*\frac{1}{3}$ (4)
- Solvency calculation:

  * If average claims ≤ 7 mln. ECU:

$$SM = \left(Z_{t-1}*26\%\right)*\frac{Sn}{Sb} \quad (5)$$

* If Average claims > 7 mln. ECU:

$$SM = \left[\left(7\text{mln. ecu} * 26\%\right) + \left(\left(Z_{t-1} - 7\text{mln. ecu}\right) * 23\%\right)\right] * \frac{Sn}{Sb} \quad (6)$$

- Requirements:

$$\frac{Sn}{Sb} \geq 50\% \quad (7)$$

- Exceptions:
  * Health insurance practised on a similar technical basis to that of life insurance (see B.1.3.).
  * Cyclical risk: risk of storm, hail, frost and credit risk.
    The solvency will be based on the average claims during the last 7 years instead of the last 3 years.
    In formula (4) 1/3 will change in 1/7.
  * Tourist assistance; amounts of claims paid shall be the costs born by the undertaking in respect of assistance given.

B.1.5. LIFE INSURANCE

The solvency level is based on the largest amount of:

- the minimum guarantee fund;
- solvency margin based on the mathematical reserves and/or the capital under risk.

B.1.6. MINIMUM GUARANTEE FUND

Limited company: 800.000 ECU.
Other companies: 600.000 ECU; or after permission of the supervisory authority 100.000 to 600.000 ECU.

B.1.7. SOLVENCY LEVEL BASED ON MATHEMATICAL RESERVES AND/OR CAPITAL UNDER RISK

The calculation of the solvency depends on the type of life insurance (risk profiles). There are 5 groups.

Group A: No unit-linked insurance (life/annuities)

- Solvency calculation:

$$SM = \left[4\% R_{w,b;br}(t) * \frac{R_{w,n}^{(t-1)}}{R_{w,b;br}^{(t-1)}}\right] + \left[0,3\% K_{r,b}(t) * \frac{K_{r,n}^{(t-1)}}{K_{r,b}^{(t-1)}}\right] \quad (8)$$

first component   : investment risk and underwriting risk;
second component : underwriting risk (death risk).

- Requirements:

$$\frac{R_{w.n}}{R_{w,b;br}} \geq 85\% \quad (9)$$

$$\frac{K_{r,n}}{K_{r,b}} \geq 50\% \quad (10)$$

- Exceptions:
  * short term risk insurance (short term life insurance)
  * less underwriting risk; changes in formula (8):
    not 0,3% but 0,1%   if duration ≤ 3 year
    not 0,3% but 0,15%   if duration between 3 and 5 years

Group B: Complementary insurance (accident, health, etc.)
See paragraph B.1.3. Solvency level based on premiums. There is no exception for the health insurance.

Group C: Capitalisation; permanent health insurance not subject to cancellation. No capital under risk, only mathematical reserves.

- Solvency calculation:

$$SM = 4\% R_{w,b;br}(t) * \frac{R_{w,n}^{(t-1)}}{R_{w,b;br}^{(t-1)}} \quad (11)$$

- Investment risk and underwriting risk.
- Requirement:

$$\frac{R_{w.n}}{R_{w,b;br}} \geq 85\% \quad (12)$$

Group D: Tontines

- Solvency calculation:

$$SM = 1\% * \text{assets of the tontines} \quad (13)$$

Group E: Unit-linked insurance and management of pension funds
There is not always an investment risk for life insurance.

- Solvency calculation:

$$SM = \left[4\% R_{w,b;br}(t) * \frac{R_{w,n}^{(t-l)}}{R_{w,b;br}^{(t-l)}} \right] + \left[1\% R_{w,b;gbr}(t) * \frac{R_{w,n}^{(t-l)}}{R_{w,b;br}^{(t-l)}} \right] + \left[0,3\% K_{r,b}(t) * \frac{K_{r,n}^{(t-l)}}{K_{r,b}^{(t-l)}} \right] \quad (14)$$

Component 1: with investment risk
Component 2: without investment risk
Component 3: with underwriting risk (death risk)

- Requirements:

$$\frac{R_{w,n}}{R_{w,b}} \geq 85\% \quad (15)$$

$$\frac{K_{r,n}}{K_{r,b}} \geq 50\% \quad (16)$$

B.2. COMPONENTS OF SOLVENCY

B.2.1. NON-LIFE INSURANCE

Table 2.1: Real solvency margin 1-1-75 until 1-7-94[26].

Real solvency margin 1-1-75 until 1-7-94	% SM.
1 paid up share capital/ **effective initial fund**	100%
2 share capital not yet paid/ **effective initial fund not yet paid** (if < 75% of capital)	50%
3 (statutory and free) reserves	100%
4 carry-forward of profits	100%
5 **supplementary contribution**[27]	50%
6 *any hidden reserves resulting from under-estimation of assets or over-estimation of liabilities (-)*	100%
7 over-estimation of technical reserve[28] (-)	20%

---

[26] First non-life directive OJEC 73/239/EEC.
[27] 1/2 ₊ (maximum contributions - contributions actually called in)
[28] Calculation method:
0.75 * ((minimum percentage * premiums) - technical reserves per contract).

Table 2.2: Real solvency margin from 1-7-94.

Real solvency margin from 1-7-94	% SM.
1 paid up share capital/ **effective initial fund and <u>members' account</u> (+)**	100%
2 share capital not yet paid/ **effective initial fund not yet paid** (if < 75% of capital)	50%
3 (statutory and free) reserves	100%
4 carry-forward of profits	100%
5 **supplementary contribution**	50%
6 *any hidden reserves resulting from under-estimation of assets*	*100%*
8 * cumulative preferential share capital (total)(+)	50%
* fixed term cumulative preferential share capital (+)	12,5%
* subordinated loan (total)(+)	50%
* subordinated loan with a fixed maturity (+)	12,5%
9 securities with no specifies maturity date and other instruments issued by the insurer(+)	50%

Italic= after permission of the supervisory authority

Bold elements: extra or substitute elements for a mutual company
(-) component no longer permitted in the third directive
(+) new components in the third directive

B.2.2. LIFE INSURANCE

Table 2.3: Real solvency margin 1-1-75 until 1-7-94[29] .

Real solvency margin 1-1-75 until 1-7-94	% SM.
1 paid up share capital/ **paid up funds of a mutual**	100%
2 share capital not yet paid/ **fund of a mutual not yet paid** (if < 75% of capital)	50%
3 (statutory and free) reserves	100%
4 carry-forward of profits	100%
5 *profit reserves[30]*	*100%*
6 *future profits*	*50%*
7 *hidden reserves resulting from the under-estimation of assets and over-estimation of liabilities other than mathematical reserves*	*100%*
8 *hidden reserves resulting from the non-Zillmerized or partially Zillmerized mathematical reserves[31]*	*100%*

[29] First life directive OJEC 79/267/EEC.
[30] Average annual profit for last 5 years * average maturity of contract
[31] Difference between non-or-partially Zillmerized mathematical reserves and Zillmerized mathematical reserves
But: difference ≤ 3,5% (capital - mathematical reserves - undepreciated acquisition costs)per policy.

Table 2.4: Real solvency margin from 1-7-94[32].

Real solvency margin from 1-7-94	% SM.
1 paid up share capital/ **paid up funds of a mutual and <u>members' account</u>** (+)	100%
2 share capital not yet paid/ **fund of a mutual not yet paid**	50%
(if < 75% of capital)	50%
3 (statutory and free) reserves	100%
4 carry-forward of profits	100%
5 *profit reserves*	*50%*
6 *future profits*	*100%*
7 *hidden reserves resulting from the under-estimation of assets and over-estimation of liabilities other than mathematical reserves*	*100%*
8 *hidden reserves resulting from the non-Zillmerized or partially Zillmerized mathematical reserves*	*100%*
9 * cumulative preferential share capital (total)(+)	50%
* fixed term cumulative preferential share capital (+)	12,5%
* subordinated loan (total)(+)	50%
* subordinated loan with a fixed maturity (+)	12,5%
10 securities with no specifies maturity date and other instruments issued by the insurer(+)	50%

Italic= after permission of the supervisory authority

Bold elements: extra or substitute elements for a mutual company
(-) component no longer permitted in the third directive
(+) new components in the third directive

B.3. **LIST OF SYMBOLS**

$K_{r,b}$: total capital under risk gross of re-insurance;

$K_{r,n}$: total capital under risk retained as the undertaking's liability after re-insurance cessions and retrocessions;

$R_{w,b;br}$: mathematical reserves relating to direct business gross of re-insurance cessions and to re-insurance acceptances as far as the insurance company bears an investment risk;

$R_{w,b;gbr}$: mathematical reserves relating to direct business gross of re-insurance cessions and to re-insurance acceptancestotal capital as far as the insurance company bears no investment risk;

$R_{w,n}$: mathematical reserves relating to direct business;

[32]   Third life directive OJEC 92/96/EEC.

Sb   :   gross amount of claims

SM   :   solvency margin

Sn   :   amount of claims remaining to be borne by the insurance company
                 after deduction of transfers for re-insurance

X_{t-1} :   amount of premiums in year $_{t-1}$ relating to direct insurance and re-
                 insurance

Y_{t-1} :   amount of claims paid during the reference period

Z_{t-1} :   average amount of claims paid during the reference period

Appendix 5.C.

Comparison of own funds

Table 3.1: elements of the own funds.

(1)	(2) Elements of the own funds	(3) non-life insurance	(4) life insurance	(5) credit institution
		maximum % of solvency		
1	paid up share capital	100%	100%	100%
	effective initial fund and members' account	100%	100%	
2	share capital not yet paid	50%	50%	-
	effective initial fund not yet paid (if < 75% of capital)	50%	50%	
3	(statutory and free) reserves[33]	100%	100%	100%
4	revaluation reserves	100%	100%	50%
5	carry-forward of profits	100%	100%	100%
6	**supplementary contribution**	50%	-	-
7	*any hidden reserves resulting from under-estimation of assets*	*100%*	-	-
8	* cumulative preferential share capital (total)	50%	50%	50%
	* fixed term cumulative preferential share capital	12,5%	12,5%	25%
	* subordinated loan (total)	50%	50%	25%
	* subordinated loan with a fixed maturity	12,5%	12,5%	-
9	securities of indeterminate duration and other instruments that fulfil the conditions required[34]	50%	50%	50%
10	*profit reserves*	-	*100%*	-
11	*future profits*	-	*100%*	-
12	*hidden reserves resulting from the under-estimation of assets and over-estimation of liabilities other than mathematical reserves*	-	*100%*	-
13	*hidden reserves resulting from the non-Zillmerized or partially Zillmerized mathematical reserves*	-	*100%*	-
14	share premium accounts	-	-	100%
15	funds for general banking	-	-	100%
16	value adjustments of credit institutions' loans and advances, debt securities, shares and other variable-yield securities which are not held as financial fixed assets.	-	-	50%
17	capital elements that fulfil certain conditions[35]	-	-	50%
18	commitments of the members (cooperative societies) commitments of the borrower (credit institution organized as funds)	-	-	25% 25%
19	own shares at book value	-	-	*
20	intangible assets	-	-	*
21	material losses of the current financial year	-	-	*
22	* holdings in other credit and financial institutions ≥ 10% of their capital	-	-	
	* subordinated loans and instruments mentioned in point 6 ≥ 10% own capital.			*
23	a. holdings in other credit and financial institutions ≤ 10% their capital	-	-	*
	b. subordinated claims and instruments mentioned in point 6 (other than mentioned in point 22) ≥ 10% own capital. (23a + 23b) - (10% of the sum of points 1, 3, 4, 5, 8, 9, 14, 15, 16, 17 and 18)			

[33] Without revaluation reserves.
[34] See OJEC 89/299/EEC, article 3, point 2.
[35] See OJEC 89/299/EEC; article 3, point 1.

Symbols:

Bold	: extra or substitute elements for a mutual company
*	: correction factor
Italic	: after permission of the supervisory authority

6. Research into the possibility of a global approach for the calculation of the solvency requirements of financial conglomerates

L.A.A. Van den Berghe
J. Roos
Erasmus Finance & Insurance Centre (NL)
De Vlerick School voor Management (B)

6.1. SOME THEORETICAL REMARKS

Financial conglomerates combine banking and insurance activities within one group. From the analysis in chapter 5 it is clear that a global approach for the calculation of the solvency requirements for financial conglomerates is not straightforward. Due to large differences in the activities involved, the accounting principles used, the legal requirements etc., it is not easy to develop a common measure for all risks involved.
It is often stated that the calculation of such a global solvency can easily be solved, by stating that the group should have the combined solvency of the constituting enterprises. Although this may be a solution in the short run, it is certainly not a sufficient one from a conceptual perspective. This aspect will be dealt with in paragraph 6.1.1.

The increased integration of banking, insurance and investment activities leads to a "blurring of the boundaries" on a product level as well as on an institutional level. The question is raised whether the solvency calculation for insurance companies should not be amended to take into consideration the "increased" investment risks, run by insurance companies. The reverse remark, that banks should also integrate "insurance risks" into their solvency calculation has not been made, to our opinion. This can certainly be explained by the fact that banks must always set up a separate company to carry their "insurance risks", whereas insurance companies can offer certain savings products within their insurance corporation.

The analysis of this question will be dealt with in paragraph 6.1.2.

The blurring of the boundaries between insurance companies and other financial institutions has also attracted the attention to the comparison of the levels of solvency needed and the calculation of the solvency fund. This comparison has led sometimes to the belief that the levels of solvency requirements for insurance companies are too low. Especially the fact that the minimum solvency requirements are much lower and that insurers do not take (sufficient) "asset risk" into consideration has been brought into the discussion. Therefore we tried to compare not only the theoretical aspects of the solvency requirements but we made also some simulation exercises to compare the levels of solvency requirements. This analysis is detailed in paragraph 6.2.

6.1.1. DO FINANCIAL CONGLOMERATES LEAD TO A DECREASING OR TO AN INCREASING ENTREPRENEURIAL RISK?

The formation of financial conglomerates is mostly based on the potential synergies and economies of scale and scope that such an integration can procure. Consequently this can eventually lead to a smaller risk and a decrease in the capital needs.
On the contrary, if economies of scale and scope can not be proven and the risks are not neutralising but strengthening each other, then it is clear that the solvency needs of financial conglomerates should be larger than the sum of the combined requirements.

Prior to any separate regulation of the solvency for financial conglomerates it is therefore necessary to make an in-depth analysis of the theoretical as well as the practical aspects of the measurement of economies and diseconomies of scale and scope for financial conglomerates in general and of the "global" risks involved more specifically. This research goes far beyond the scope of this publication. The Erasmus University has given us the opportunity to study this topic into greater detail in the near future.

6.1.2. DOES THE SOLVENCY REQUIREMENTS OF INSURANCE COMPANIES NEED AN UPGRADING TO TAKE ALSO THE "ASSET" RISKS INTO ACCOUNT ?

This question will be dealt with in greater detail in paragraph 6.2. The more theoretical aspects will be analysed here.

It has been explained in chapter 5 that the solvency calculation for insurance companies mainly focuses on the underwriting risk.
The risks involved with the investments of their technical provisions are monitored through a double regulation:

- the regulation of the investment policy: diversification of the portfolio, limitation of the investments per category of assets and per creditor;
- accounting rules and prescriptions for the evaluation of the "representative" assets.

For life insurance companies also the investment risk is taken into account in the calculation of the required solvency level. The evolution towards unit linked products and innovative combinations of investment, savings and life insurance products does not lead automatically to more investment risk for the insurer. In fact two opposing trends can be observed in this respect:

- at the one hand the increased competition stresses the need for more competitive "guaranteed" returns; this was especially the case for life insurance contracts with an important saving element; these products can lead to an increased investment risk for the insurers;
- on the other hand, the increased competition was at the origin of a numerous set of innovations; quite a lot of these modern life insurance products give a substantial part or even the complete investment return to the clients; in these cases the investment risk is no longer carried by the insurer himself but by the client.

6.2. SIMULATIONS OF THE COMBINED SOLVENCY

The statistical comparison of the level of solvency required for banks and insurance companies raises some specific problems.

Since the banks do not have "underwriting" variables such as premiums, claims and capital under risk, the measures used for the insurance companies cannot be applied to the banking sector.

The reverse can be done more easily. Nevertheless the banking rules could not be copied completely. Quite a number of assumptions had to be made. This is logical, since there is always a clear interaction between the regulations, the accounting rules and the business practice. The regulations determine the accounting rules and set the boundaries for the business activities. It has been observed in several respects, that regulations can lead to corrections and adaptations in the business activities, not only to stay within the boundaries set out by the regulatory environment, but also to circumvent some of the limitations set by the regulations. The off-balance sheet activities are an interesting element in this respect; but also the use of subordinated loans or of reinsurance (for insurance companies) can be instructive to learn more about the dynamics of regulations.

Therefore we limited our simulation exercises to the application of the banking rules to insurance companies. These simulations were based on four Dutch insurance companies[1] detailed annual accounts. We included life as well as non-life companies into the sample and also larger and smaller companies.

Before analysing the results of these simulations in greater detail, we first want to stress the main problems encountered in calculating the required solvency level (paragraph 6.2.1) and the solvency funds (paragraph 6.2.2).

6.2.1. THE CALCULATION OF THE REQUIRED SOLVENCY LEVEL FOR INSURERS ON THE BASIS OF THE BANKING RULES

The definition of the required solvency level is based on several variables that can not be found directly in the detailed annual accounts of insurance companies, so that the following assumptions had to be made:

- types of creditors:
  since the annual accounts of insurance companies are not detailed in the same way as those of credit institutions, simply copying the banking rules is not possible. For some categories of assets the analogy with banking accounts poses no problem. Other elements, especially insurance related elements, pose more problems. We will only summarize the most specific aspects (appendix 6.A. gives more details in this respect):
  * typical insurance variables such as "participation of reinsurers in the technical provisions", "deposits with reinsurers", "policy loans" and "interest rate rebates" do need special attention; some elements do not carry that much risk (e.g. policy loans) while others can be more risky (e.g. deposits with non-supervised reinsurers in exotic fiscal paradises);
  * the relations with other financial institutions: different hypotheses can be defended (see appendix 6.A.); it is our belief that those relations can be interpreted as "intra-sectoral" so that the same weighting factor (of 20%) must be applied; this analogy only holds in as far as the institutions under consideration are subject to strict supervision;
  * certain categories of investment that can have a public character: e.g. utility firms; a distinction will therefore be necessary between public and private sectors (or percentage of publicly or privately owned).
  The analysis of the impact of the different assumptions in relation to the above mentioned variables (see appendix 6.B.) showed that the relative weight of these factors is quite different. Especially the relations with other financial institutions is important.
- types of countries:
  the allocation of countries to Zone A, respectively Zone B is based on "confi-

---

[1]   The figures are derived from the official annual accounts for 1992, made up for the supervisory authorities so that the reference base is the "working company" (non-consolidated accounts).

dential" information; we assumed therefore that all OECD countries are part of Zone A, while all other countries belong to Zone B;
- Off-Balance Sheet transactions (OBS):
  are not recorded separately in the annual accounts of insurance companies; inquiries with the companies in question learned that these activities have been of no importance in the past (there was no reward nor penalty for such activities); it is however clear that there is a growing interest, especially within integrated financial conglomerates, to use some of the modern derivatives and off-balance sheet instruments more frequently (especially as a financial risk management vehicle).

6.2.2. THE CALCULATION OF THE SOLVENCY FUND FOR INSURERS ON THE BASIS OF THE BANKING RULES

The distinction between tier 1 and tier 2 capital can be made without significant difficulties. Certain important differences can however be observed:

- the impact of subordinated loans is much less important in the insurance sector; this is not astonishing, since those elements were previously not accepted as solvency funds; this again proves that there is a dynamic interaction between the regulatory environment and the business practices;
- the elimination of double gearing (cross shareholding) is possible in as far as the own funds are calculated on a "net basis";
- the relative importance of capital gains and implicit elements is far greater in insurance companies than it is the case for banks; this can certainly be explained by the greater degree of uncertainty in relation to the "annual" accounting of the profitability of the business written and the technical reservations needed.
  From the statistics in appendix 6.B. we can learn that the impact of these elements is very important in the life sector; especially older and "orthodox" insurers have built up considerable reserves in this respect. This was especially clear for company "NL" (see appendix 6.B., table 2.5). This company has such large "revaluation reserves" that these elements cannot be included completely as solvency funds. This can be explained by the fact that these reserves are interpreted - according to the strict application of the banking rules - as tier 2 capital and this tier can never exceed the tier 1 capital.

6.2.3. ANALYSIS OF THE SIMULATION RESULTS

- Applying the banking rules to the insurance companies:
  The calculation of the solvency margin for the four insurance companies, on the basis of the banking rules, leads to the following conclusions:
  * the minimum solvency or guarantee requirements are met by all insurance

companies;
* 3 of the 4 companies studied have a solvency margin which is by far greater than needed according to the banking rules; the only exception is the company that has so large "revaluation reserves" that only part of this reserve can be considered as tier 2 capital; if all the reserves could be included, the solvency margin would increase from 7 to 13% (see appendix 6.B., table 2.5);
* the application of the solvency requirements of banks to the four insurance companies resulted in 3 of the 4 cases in amounts that were even smaller than the ones prescribed by the insurance authorities (see appendix 6.B., table 2.6))

Comparing the different companies studied learns that the impact of applying the banking rules to the insurance sector has rather different effects whether the company under consideration is a life or a non-life company. A non-life company is not a "financial intermediary" in the strict sense of the word, but the function of institutional investor is only induced through the insurance "capitalisation" technique and the "inversion of the exploitation cycle". Due to the relative "shorter term" of their commitments, the investment policy primarily focuses on liquidity; their assets have a lower risk profile and consequently need less solvency capital. Life insurers, on the contrary, focus more on return in the long term; a higher return is often associated with higher risks, so that their solvency needs, calculated on the basis of the "weighted assets" is considerably higher.

This difference is even more pronounced if only the investments are taken into consideration (compare table 2.1 and 2.2 in appendix 6.B.).

If we compare this observation with the underwriting experience, than it becomes clear that the banking rules are not very useful for non-life companies. From a pure insurance perspective, the non-life business is far more risky than the life business.

The difference between larger and smaller companies is also important to mention. The larger the groups are the more sophisticated their financial management is. Consequently their assets tend to contain more risky elements, but at the same time the diversification degree is also quite larger. The application of the banking rules leads to a relatively higher solvency need for larger companies. This is again in contrast with the solvency measures, based on the underwriting risks. It can be proven, on the basis of the law of large numbers, that the underwriting risks of larger portfolios can be estimated more accurately than for smaller portfolios; consequently the solvency requirements for non-life companies are degressive, which means that larger companies have proportionally less solvency needs than smaller ones.

- Combining the solvency calculations of banks with those of insurance companies:

We already observed that the question is sometimes raised whether the solvency requirements for insurance companies should not be upgraded to incorporate also the "asset risks". We therefore calculated also the solvency level for insurance companies combining the requirements of the "insurance" regulations with those of the "banking" sector.

Such a combination however is "overshooting" the required solvency level, certainly in the case of life insurance companies. We can prove this hypothesis on the following grounds:

* the life insurance regulations already integrate considerable solvency requirements to cover the "investment risk"; as explained in chapter 5, the investment risk included in the solvency calculation, can be deducted from the comparison of the requirements for "classical" life insurance products with those for "unit linked" products (with no investment risk for the insurer); the first category needs 4% of the mathematical reserves, while the latter only needs 1%; consequently the difference (3%) represents the investment risks;

    the solvency needs, calculated on the basis of the "weighted" asset risks, should therefore be corrected for the investment risk already integrated in the "insurance solvency calculations";

* the application of the "corrected" banking rules to the life insurance companies of our sample must start from certain hypotheses in relation to the "risk indicators"; it is therefore not possible to make absolute statements on the level of solvency required; from our calculation it is however clear that in most cases the insurance solvency calculations take MORE investment risk into consideration than the corresponding measures for the banking sector; it is therefore clear that the life insurance measures are probably not underestimating the investment risk!!!! (see appendix 6.B., table 2.7a and table 2.7b).

6.3. ANALYSIS OF THE NEED FOR AN ACTUALISATION OF THE MINIMUM SOLVENCY REQUIREMENTS

Discussions have developed whether the minimum solvency requirements should not be updated to take into account the depreciation of the monetary value. This is especially questioned for the "older" definitions, such as non-life insurance (dates back to 1973) or life insurance (1979). The directives for credit institutions are from a more recent date (1989).

We therefore studied the potential effect of inflation on a European level and the influence of both inflation and exchange rate differences for the Dutch market (as a case study).

The details of this analysis are given in appendix 6.C. We limit the discussion here to the conclusions.

On the European level, it could be argued that the minimum solvency requirements must be corrected to take into account the "EU-inflation". According to the difference in reference year, the correction must be the largest for the non-life branches (more than 3 times the actual level), followed by the life branches (more than the double of the actual level); only minor changes will be needed for the banking sector.

The impact of these changes will be different in each member state, according to the evolution of their currency rate against the ECU and to their specific inflationary experience. For the Netherlands the impact would be lower than the average EU-adaptations, mentioned before. This can be explained by the fact that the Dutch economy performed better than the EU-average and had a lower inflation rate over the period under consideration. The potential correction would be the following:

-   for the non-life branches: x 2,25
-   for the life branches: x 1,5
-   for the credit institutions: x 1,13.

More details can be found in appendix 6.C., table 3.4.

Appendix 6.A.

Theoretical problems in the application of the banking rules to insurance companies

A.1. **DEFINITION OF THE SOLVENCY NEEDED: THE WEIGHTING FACTORS**

Specific insurance variables:

- Assets in relation to reinsurance contracts.
  The two most important assets that can be related to reinsurance contracts are the following:
  * participation of reinsurers in the technical provisions;
  * deposit with reinsurers;
  If the definition of the banking sector is translated to the insurance sector, such elements should be interpreted as "intra sectoral relationships". Since the specialised reinsurers are not supervised to the same extent as direct insurers and mixed (direct - /re -insurers) insurers are, a distinction must certainly be made in this respect. For the "supervised" reinsurers a 20% weighting factor is analogous to the banking directive; for the "non-supervised" ones a higher weighting factor will be necessary[2].
- Policy loans.
  This is a form of disintermediation and contains little or no investment or credit risk.
- Interest rate rebates.
  In order to offer a competitive product, life insurers have increased the return of their contracts not only by adding extra profit participations above the "actuarial interest rate", but they also decreased their premium or rate by discounting for the future extra investment return. This up-front discount is then depreci-

---

[2]   Due to changes in the accounting rules the "participation of reinsurers" will have to be deducted from the technical provisions (liabilities), so that no "asset" variable will be mentioned any longer. However, the risks eventually associated with this "asset" still remain the same.

ated over a period of time. This activated variable does not contain that much risk in as far as the "matching" of liabilities and assets is good or in as far as the eventual reinvestment risk is taken into account. Such an asset element will therefore not need a high weighting factor[3]. Due to changes in the accounting rules the "interest rate rebates" will be deducted from the technical provisions (liabilities), so that no "asset" variable will be mentioned any longer.

Relations with other financial firms:

- The banking directive recognizes that relations with other credit institutions (or Zone A countries) do not entail great risks, so that the weighting factor is 20%. The extrapolation of these principles to the calculation of the solvency require- ments for insurance companies can be based on three hypotheses:
  * hypothesis 1:
    a strict application of the banking rules leads to the conclusion that only "credit institutions" can benefit from this 20% rule, while all other financial firms have to be treated as any other non-financial firm (100% weighting factor);
  * hypothesis 2:
    the opposite picture could be defended for the calculation of the solvency requirements for insurance companies on the grounds that "intra-sectoral" relationships can only mean that insurance companies benefit from the 20% rule, while all other financial firms are to be treated as non-financial firms (100% rule);
  * hypothesis 3:
    adaptation of the banking rules to the "regulated" and "supervised" insur- ance sectors leads to the conclusion that all financial institutions (that are under strict supervision) benefit from a parallel solvency rule (20% weight- ing factor).

These three hypotheses will be used in the simulation exercises in appendix 6.B.

- Investments in utility firms.
  Some utility firms are publicly owned while others are partly or wholly private. The weighting factors for public firms are much lower than for private firms. An accurate application of the banking rules will not be possible as long as no distinction is made in this respect .

---

[3]   Due to changes in the accounting rules the "interest rate rebates" will have to be deducted from the technical provisions (liabilities), so that no "asset" variable will be mentioned any longer. However, the risks eventually associated with this "asset" still remain the same.

Appendix 6.B.

Simulation exercises

Cases studied:

LS   : smaller non-life insurer
LL   : smaller life insurer
RS   : larger non-life insurer
NL   : large life insurer

B.1. CALCULATION OF THE SOLVENCY REQUIRED ACCORDING TO THE BANKING DIRECTIVES

Table 2.1: The "total assets" per risk category and their relative importance.

(1) assets (%)	(2) LS	(3) LL	(4) RS	(5) NL
wf: 0%	39,22	28,08	46,77	14,00
wf: 20%	28,64	41,14	40,23	21,76
wf: 50%	12,84	15,10	3,98	19,03
wf: 100%	12,74	10,81	6,55	37,34
wf: variable	6,56	4,87	2,47	7,85

Table 2.2: The "investment" components per risk category and their relative importance.

(1) investments	(2) LS	(3) LL	(4) RS	(5) NL
wf: 0%	50,13	31,24	49,62	18,17
wf: 20%	34,33	44,82	42,68	28,04
wf: 50%	12,69	12,90	0,00	22,08
wf: 100%	2,85	8,74	6,91	29,69
wf: variable	0,00	2,30	0,79	2,02

Table 2.3: Share of insurers and credit institutions as counterparty.

(1) percentage of the balance sheet total (excl. provisions)	(2) LS	(3) LL	(4) RS	(5) NL
insurers	0,61	1,85	4,48	7,03
participation of reinsurers in the technical provisions	6,56	0,59	1,70	2,94
deposit with reinsurers	0,00	0,00	0,02	1,39
total insurers	**7,17**	**2,44**	**6,2**	**11,36**
credit institutions wf 20%	**7,99**	**17,13**	**27,57**	**9,09**
credit institutions wf 100%	0,00	0,00	0,4	0,53

Table 2.4: Simulation of the solvency ratio of insurance companies on the basis of the three hypotheses mentioned.

(1)	(2) LS	(3) LL	(4) RS	(5) NL
hypothesis 1	105,5	33,4	166,7	6,4
hypothesis 2	103,3	23,4	86,5	6,6
hypothesis 3	129,0	35,9	228,1	7,7

hypothesis 1:
a strict application of the banking rules leads to the conclusion that only "credit institutions" can benefit from the 20% rule, while all other financial firms have to be treated as any other non-financial firm (100% weighting factor);

hypothesis 2:
the opposite picture could be defended for the calculation of the solvency requirements for insurance companies on the grounds that "intra-sectoral" relationships can only mean that insurance companies benefit from the 20% rule, while all other financial firms are to be treated as non-financial firms (100% rule);

hypothesis 3:
adaptation of the banking rules to the "regulated" and "supervised" insurance sectors leads to the conclusion that all financial institutions (that are under strict supervision) benefit from a parallel solvency rule (20% weighting factor);

Table 2.5: The solvency according to the banking directive.

(1) (* f1000)	(2) LS	(3) LL	(4) RS	(5) NL
1. required solvency (bank directive): weighted assets * 8%	2807	15563	3348	2675946
2. components of solvency				
tier 1	46019	53847	50426	1166208
tier 2 (limited)	765	12443	26553	1166208
total a	46784	66290	76979	2332416
tier 2 (unlimited)	765	12443	26553	3374979
total b	46784	66290	76979	4541187
3. solvency margin				
total a / required solvency	133,3	34	184	7
total b / required solvency	133,3	34	184	13

Table 2.6: The required solvency according to the insurance and banking rules.

(1) (* f1000)	(2) LS	(3) LL	(4) RS	(5) NL
1. required solvency (bank directive) weighted assets * 8%	2807	15563	3348	2675946
2. required solvency (ins. directive)	8365	31852	30019	2209788

B.2. COMBINING SOLVENCY REQUIREMENTS ACCORDING TO INSURANCE AND BANKING RULES

Table 2.7a: The required solvency according to insurance and banking rules together (minimum weighting factors for certain variables[4]).

(1) (* f 1000)	(2) LS	(3) LL	(4) NL	(5) RS
technical provisions				
# including investment risk		23203	1729996	
# excluding investment risk		67	65253	
risk under capital		8227	377901	
solvency based on premium	8365	355	36638	30019
solvency based on claims	5755			21463
1. Required solvency; insurance rules	8365	a) 31852	2209788	30019
minimum guarantee fund	1448	1770	1770	1448
2. Required solvency banking rules	2807	15563	2675946	3348
initial capital	11060	11060	11060	11060
3 (A). Required solvency (insurance and banking rules)	19425	47415	4885734	41079
sum of the minimum guarantee fund and the initial capital	12508	12830	12830	12508
3 (B). Required solvency (insurance and banking rules)	11172	47415	4885734	33367
sum of the minimum guarantee fund and the initial capital	12508	12830	12830	12508
4. Correction investment risk (insurance rules)				
A.method 1 (EU rules)		-17402	-1297497	
total solvency		a) 30013	3588237	
B. method 2 (Dutch rules)		-17344	-1279476	
total solvency		30071	3606258	

[4] These variables are:
- participations of reinsurers in the technical reserves;
- deposits with reinsurers;
- policy loans;
- interest rates rebates;
- relations with other financial institutions;
- investments that can have a public character.

Table 2.7b: The required solvency according to insurance and banking rules together (maximum weighting factors for certain variables[5]).

(1) (∗ fl 1000)	(2) LS	(3) LL	(4) NL	(5) RS
technical provisions				
# including investment risk		23203	1729996	
# excluding investment risk		67	65253	
risk under capital		8227	377901	
solvency based on premium	8365	355	36638	30019
solvency based on claims	5755			21463
1. **Required solvency; insurance rules**	**8365**	*b)* **31852**	**2209788**	**30019**
minimum guarantee fund	1448	1770	1770	1448
2. **Required solvency; banking rules**	*3547*	**18151**	**3073091**	*3813*
initial capital	*11060*	11060	11060	*11060*
3 **(A). Required solvency (insurance and banking rules)**	**19425**	**50003**	**5282879**	**41079**
sum of the minimum guarantee fund and the initial capital	12508	12830	12830	12508
3 **(B). Required solvency (insurance and banking rules)**	**11912**	**50003**	**5282879**	**33832**
sum of the minimum guarantee fund and the initial capital	12508	12830	12830	12508
4. **Correction investment risk (insurance rules)**				
method 1 (EU rules)			-17402	-1297497
total solvency		*b)*	*32601*	3985382
method 2 (Dutch rules)			-17344	-1279476
total solvency			32659	4003403

Remarks table 2.7a and 2.7b:

- The required solvency for the non-life insurers comes below the initial capital. Method A: sum of the required solvency (insurance rules) and the initial capital.
  Method B: sum of the required solvency (insurance rules) and the required solvency (banking rules)
  Which method is the right one?

---

[5] These variables are:
  - participations of reinsurers in the technical reserves;
  - deposits with reinsurers;
  - policy loans;
  - interest rates rebates;
  - relations with other financial institutions;
  - investments that can have a public character.

- In table 2.7a. the solvency corrected for investment risk for LL comes below the required solvency according to the insurance rules ([a]). This is not the case in table 2.7b ([b]). So, it is important that the variables get the right weighting factor.
- Correction investment risk (insurance rules)
  method 1 (EU rules):

$$\left(4\% - 1\%\right) * R_{w,b;br} * \left[\frac{R_{w,n}}{R_{w,b;br}}\right]$$

method 2 (Dutch rules):

$$\left(4\% * R_{w,b;br} * \left[\frac{R_{w,n}}{R_{w,b;br}}\right]\right) - \left(1\% * R_{w,b;gbr}\right)$$

Unit-linked insurance and management of pension funds; solvency calculation according to Dutch rules.

$$SM = \left[4\% R_{w,b;br}(t) * \frac{R_{w,n}^{(t-1)}}{R_{w,b;br}^{(t-1)}}\right] + \left[1\% R_{w,b;gbr}(t)\right] + \left[0,3\% K_{r,b}(t) * \frac{K_{r,n}^{(t-1)}}{K_{r,b}^{(t-1)}}\right]$$

Appendix 6.C.

Correction: minimum solvency levels

Table 3.1: Value ECU in Dutch guilders.

Year	Value ECU in Dutch guilders	
non-life insurance	ƒ 3.62	(ecu old)
1979	ƒ 2,76	(ecu old)
1989	ƒ 2,32	(ecu old)
1993	ƒ 2,15	(ecu new)

For the consumer price indices of EU countries and the EU, see page 18.

C.1. CORRECTION ON THE EUROPEAN LEVEL

Table 3.2: The minimum solvency level corrected for inflation (in ecu).

(1) MS corrected by CPI	(2) MS	(3) multiplication factor = (1)/(2)
non-life insurance (1973).		
612896	200000	3.06
919344	300000	3.06
1225792	400000	3.06
1781805	1400000	1.27[6]
life insurance (1979)		
203290	100000	2.03
406580	200000	2.03
609871	300000	2.03
813161	400000	2.03
1016451	500000	2.03
1219741	600000	2.03
1626322	800000	2.03
credit institutions (1989)		
1176918	1000000	1.18
2353837	2000000	1.18
3530755	3000000	1.18
4707674	4000000	1.18
5884592	5000000	1.18

[6]   1987 instead of 1973

Table 3.3: The minimum solvency corrected for the consumer price index and the change in the value of the ECU (in Dutch guilders).

(1) year	(2) MS (in ecu)	(3) MS (ecu=old)	(4) MS (ecu=old) corrected by CPI$_{NL}$	(5) multiplication factor =(4/3)
		in Dutch guilders		
	non-life insurance	ecu = f3,62		1973=1
1973	200000	724000	1650461.2	2.28
1973	300000	1086000	2475691.8	2.28
1973	400000	1448000	3300922.4	2.28
1987	1400000	5068000	8259414.0	1.63[7]
	life insurance	ecu = f2,76		1979=1
1979	100000	275779	415389.9	1.51
1979	200000	551558	830779.7	1.51
1979	300000	827337	1246169.6	1.51
1979	400000	1103116	1661559.4	1.51
1979	500000	1378895	2076949.3	1.51
1979	600000	1654674	2492339.2	1.51
1979	800000	2206232	3323118.9	1.51
	credit institutions	ecu = f2,315		1989=1
1989	1000000	2315140	2608800.8	1.13
1989	2000000	4630280	5217601.7	1.13
1989	3000000	6945420	7826402.5	1.13
1989	4000000	9260560	10435203.0	1.13
1989	5000000	11575700	13044004.0	1.13

C.2. CORRECTIONS FOR THE DUTCH MARKET

Table 3.4: The minimum solvency corrected for the Dutch consumer price index.

(1) MS corrected by CPI ecu=old	(2) MS ecu=old	(3) multiplication factor =(1/2)	(4) MS corrected by CPI ecu=new	(5) MS corrected by CPI ecu=old	(6) multiplication factor =(4/5)	(7) multiplication factor (total) =(4/2)
non-life insurance			non-life insurance			
2218683	724000	3.06	1316231	2218683	0.59	1.82
3328025	1086000	3.06	1974346	3328025	0.59	1.82
4437367	1448000	3.06	2632462	4437367	0.59	1.82
6450135	5068000	1.27	3826533	6450135	0.59	0.76
life insurance			life insurance			
560632	275779	2.03	436578	560632	0.78	1.58
1121263	551558	2.03	873156	1121263	0.78	1.58
1681895	827337	2.03	1309734	1681895	0.78	1.58
2242527	1103116	2.03	1746312	2242527	0.78	1.58
2803159	1378895	2.03	2182890	2803159	0.78	1.58
3363790	1654674	2.03	2619468	3363790	0.78	1.58
4485054	2206232	2.03	3492624	4485054	0.78	1.58
credit institutions			credit institutions			
2724731	2315140	1.18	2527503	2724731	0.93	1.09
5449462	4630280	1.18	5055006	5449462	0.93	1.09
8174193	6945420	1.18	7582509	8174193	0.93	1.09
10898924	9260560	1.18	10110012	10898924	0.93	1.09
13623655	11575700	1.18	12637515	13623655	0.93	1.09

[7] 1987 = 1.

Table 3.5: Consumer price indices for EU countries and the EU.

Consumer Prices indices — $1985 = 100$

Year	B	DK	D	G	E	F	IRL	I	L	NL	P	UK	EU
1973	41.3	32.9	59.6	12.8	17.8	30.3	20.6	17.5	43.5	50.3	9.0	24.9	40.5
1974	46.6	37.9	63.7	16.1	20.6	34.5	24.1	20.9	47.2	55.1	11.3	29.2	44.8
1975	52.3	41.7	67.7	18.3	24.0	38.4	29.0	24.3	52.4	60.6	13.0	36.1	49.4
1976	57.0	45.4	70.5	20.7	28.3	42.2	34.3	28.5	57.7	66.0	15.6	42.2	53.5
1977	61.1	50.1	73.3	23.3	35.1	46.1	38.9	33.7	61.3	70.3	19.9	48.8	57.7
1978	63.9	55.5	75.3	26.3	42.0	50.3	41.9	37.8	63.2	73.3	24.4	52.8	60.9
1979	66.8	60.8	78.4	31.3	48.6	55.7	47.4	43.4	66.1	76.1	30.1	59.9	65.3
1980	71.2	68.3	82.6	39.0	56.2	63.3	56.1	52.5	70.3	81.8	35.2	70.7	72.0
1981	76.6	76.3	87.9	48.6	64.4	71.8	67.5	61.9	76.0	87.2	42.2	79.1	79.0
1982	83.3	84.0	92.5	58.7	73.7	80.3	79.1	72.1	83.1	92.2	51.8	85.9	85.7
1983	89.7	89.8	95.5	70.8	82.6	88.0	87.3	82.7	90.2	94.8	64.9	89.8	91.0
1984	95.4	95.5	97.9	83.7	91.9	94.4	94.8	91.6	95.4	97.8	83.6	94.3	95.6
1985	100.0	100.0	100.0	100.0	100.0	100.0	100.0	100.0	100.0	100.0	100.0	100.0	100.0
1986	101.3	103.6	99.9	123.0	108.8	102.7	103.8	105.8	100.3	100.2	111.7	103.4	102.1
1987	102.9	107.8	100.1	143.2	114.5	105.9	107.1	110.9	100.2	99.8	122.2	107.7	104.3
1988	104.1	112.7	101.4	162.5	120.0	108.7	109.4	116.5	101.7	100.7	133.9	113.0	107.2
1989	107.3	118.1	104.2	184.9	128.2	112.7	113.9	123.8	105.1	101.7	150.8	121.8	112.8
1990	111.0	121.2	107.0	222.6	136.8	116.5	117.6	131.8	109.0	104.3	170.9	133.3	118.3
1991	114.6	124.1	110.7	264.7	145.0	120.0	121.3	146.2	112.4	108.4	190.3	141.1	124.2
1992	117.3	126.7	115.1	308.1	153.5	123	125.1	147.3	115.9	11.7	206.7	146.4	128.5
1993	120.6	128.3	119.8	352.6	160.6	125.6	126.9	153.8	120.1	114.6	220	148.7	132.8

Explanation of the symbols:

MS   minimum solvency
CPI   consumer price index
CPI_{NL} consumer price index for The Netherlands

7. Financial conglomerates, solvency and risks

Discussion on risks and solvency

This chapter contains a discussion on risks of financial conglomerates (chapter 4) and on the solvency regulations for financial conglomerates (chapter 5 and 6, which were originally respectively paper III and paper IV in the workshop). The discussion in paragraph 7.1. and 7.2. by Simonson and Løining will concentrate on the solvency regulation in Norway. Paragraph 7.3. by J. Roos gives a short review of the risk-based capital system in the United States. Paragraph 7.4., 7.5. and 7.6. contain the discussion by respectively Holsboer, Knaut and Pearson on the chapters 4, 5 and 6.

7.1. DISCUSSION BY S. SIMONSEN[1]

7.1.1. SOLIDITY REQUIREMENTS

Quite often we are asked about the solidity requirements which apply to the Norwegian insurance companies. If we do not take care in being very precise, misunderstandings can easily occur. In particular we often see a misunderstanding of the risk connected to the insurance risk, such as underwriting risk etc. It is often believed to be covered by the 8 per cent capital adequacy rule that is generally applicable. But this is not the case. In Norway we have one set of rules that apply to the credit risk (assets) and another separate set of rules that apply to insurance risk. A short overview of the Norwegian rules can be presented as follows:

Financial legislation in Norway has been substantially revised in recent years. This applies to all types of credit institutions as well as insurance and holding companies. The capital adequacy requirements applicable to insurance companies are structured as follows:

Both insurance companies and banks (and other credit institutions) are providers of various types of credit and other financial services. Their assets are therefore exposed to a credit risk (investment risk). The credit risk attached to a loan, investment, security, etc. is the same whether the loan or the investment is made by

[1]   Senior Executive Officer at the Banking, Insurance and Securities Commission of Norway.

a bank or by an insurance company. The Norwegian capital adequacy requirements are therefore equally designed with regard to coverage of credit risk in credit institutions and insurance companies. The required capital ratio has, in accordance with the EC directives for credit institutions, been set at 8 per cent of risk weighted assets for both groups. The capital elements used to meet the 8 per cent requirement are the same for all financial institutions (including banks and insurance companies), and follow the definition of the EC directive on the own funds of credit institutions. It should be mentioned that there, in addition, are rules concerning the consolidation of financial institutions' holdings in other financial institutions (including e.g. banks and insurance companies). These rules apply accordingly both to credit institutions, insurance companies and holding companies within a financial group, both individually as well as on a consolidated basis (i.e. consolidation for the whole financial sector).

Insurance companies are exposed to other types of risks than banks, e.g. various types of insurance risks such as underwriting risk and risk related to the year-to-year fluctuations of the technical result of the insurance activity. Separate solvency requirements have been introduced to cover these kinds of risks. These requirements are different for life and non-life insurance.

Accordingly, the Norwegian solidity requirements for insurance companies consist of two parts:

-   A capital requirement covering credit (investment) risks (which is identical with the one applicable to banks). (1)
-   Technical provisions which cover underwriting risks etc. These technical provisions (requirements) vary between life and non-life insurance. (2)

These main categories of solidity requirements should be interpreted as complementary, meaning that no share of the amounts covering one of the requirements can be used to cover the other.
The Norwegian insurance companies are, in accordance with the present Norwegian legislation, obliged to meet the total requirement given by the sum of the two parts above.

Norwegian authorities are now implementing the EC directives on insurance, including the requirements for solvency margins. The solvency margins are generally calculated on the basis of the insurance obligations of the insurance companies. In the future Norway will thus have a two track system. Along one track we have the requirements given by (1) and (2) above, and along the second track the EC solvency requirements. These two sets of rules are along two different tracks and are therefore not additive.
It may also be noted that credit institutions, insurance companies and holding

companies in Norway are supervised by the same authority. This has proven to be quite advantageous although it is not a necessary condition for consolidating and applying the same capital rules for credit risk to both groups. So far we have applied these rules for four years and during this period we have not discovered any loopholes.

7.1.2. CONSOLIDATION

The capital adequacy rule not only applies to the individual company. It also applies to a group or sub-group on a consolidated basis. This is regulated in section 2a-9 in the Act[2] and in regulation given in accordance with this Act.

> "A financial institution shall, when applying rules on capital adequacy and other rules concerning financial strength and safety, consolidate the accounts when the institution directly or indirectly holds 20 per cent or more of the share capital or the votes in:
> a) another Norwegian or foreign financial institution,
> b) a Norwegian or foreign securities house, property company, investment trust company or other company with substantial financial assets.
> The obligation to undertake consolidation also applies to a financial institution which is the parent company in a sub-group, as well as to collaborating mutual insurance companies and other corresponding group affiliates which are not part of an ownership hierarchy."

The consolidation must be done according to a proportional principle. It might include ownership of 10 per cent, or more if the supervisory authority so decides.

"Double gearing" is avoided due to the sub-regulation, regulation on the measurement of the capital of financial institutions section 7 e and f, where it reads:

> "The following items shall be deducted from total capital:
> d. ......
> e. Book values of any kind for capital in other financial institutions for the part which exceeds 2 per cent of the capital in the recipient financial institutions.
> f. Book values of any kind for capital that is not deducted pursuant to litera e. above, for that part of the sum of such capital that exceeds 10 per cent of the financial institution's own capital."

7.1.3. SUPERVISION

On the supervisory side our experience is that it is a substantial advantage to have one supervisory authority which covers banks, insurance companies, holding companies and other connected companies. This makes it easier to get an overall view and to supervise financial groups as well as the financial system in general.

---

[2] See also appendix 2.A.

It should be stressed that similarities in the credit risk are not the only reason for our way of organising the supervision. It is also important to take into account the fact that we have a harmonised legislation applicable to banks and insurance companies - in addition to equal capital adequacy rules. We have the same principles for consolidation, ownership limitations etc.; which also apply to holding companies. We do apply the same supervisory technics on the similar problems, no matter if they arise in an insurance company, a holding company or a bank. Where there are differences - i.e. insurance risk for insurance companies - we do apply different supervisory technics. The supervisory authority works both on an individual basis for each company and on a consolidated basis for the group as such. Even though we have a much larger degree of similarity in our legislation for banks and insurance companies compared to most other countries - we do acknowledge that there are differences and act in accordance with this.

7.2. DISCUSSION BY Ø. LØINING[3]

We would all agree in general on the overriding importance of having a well functioning legislative framework applicable to the financial sector, including financial conglomerates or groups. It is also important that legislation is designed to establish a level playing field, i.e. an equal set of rules for all market participants.

A primary question is, however, how such a legislation is to be implemented in order to reach these goals. The implementation has proven to be subject to the power and influence of various market participants, both on the part of the financial institutions - which in my terminology include banks and insurance companies - and on the part of the authorities. For example, in those countries where there are separate supervisory authorities for banks and insurance companies, the interests of the two can be different with regard to the establishment of a joint supervisory entity.

In recent years Norway has experienced a banking crisis. With this in mind, it is natural to pose the question whether the legislation applicable to the financial sector in our country is adequate. I believe it is correct to answer this question affirmative. The experience of the past 3-5 years has shown that the financial legislation has functioned effectively and that it has been successfully implemented.

The background for the banking crisis dates back to the years 1984-1986. The crisis was, however, not apparent until the beginning of the 1990s. As early as in 1986-1987 the Norwegian financial legislation was substantially revised, with the aim of improvement. This was done at a point in time when we did not know that a

---

[3]   Deputy Director General, Ministry of Finance, Norway.

banking crisis would emerge only a few years later. New provisions related to key areas were adopted in 1988.

With regard to the key topic relating to financial conglomerates or groups (as I will call them), it is important to bear in mind that the new Norwegian legislation adopted in 1988 was supplemented by legal amendments in 1991.

A number of problems arise with regard to financial groups. Three problems in particular are:

- Intragroup transactions.
  This concerns the question of how to ensure that transactions within a group are made in accordance with ordinary business terms and principles.
- Cross-subsidisation.
  The aim is to ensure that companies in a group, or an activity within a company, do not subsidise other companies or other activities in the same company. This problem is particularly liable to occur when a company is exposed to little competition. In such a situation it may be in a position to subsidise another company within the group (or an activity within the same company), which is exposed to a greater degree of competition. I think it is fair to say that this problem mainly applies to the life insurance sector, although it may also be a more general problem.

Point 1 and 2 above cover what is generally referred to as conflicts of interest.

- Different capital requirements including the problem of double gearing. The credit risk associated with a loan or an investment is the same whether it has been made by a bank or an insurance company. If, for example, a normal credit is extended to a private enterprise (e.g. with the risk weight of 100% in the capital adequacy requirements for banks) the risk attached to this credit must be the same whether it is granted by a bank or an insurance company. The same would be the case for similar investments in securities. This is the primary reason why Norway has applied the same capital adequacy requirements to the asset side of both credit institutions and insurance companies.

Equal capital adequacy requirements are also essential in the creation of a level playing field, where the different financial institutions are compelled to compete on equal terms in the provision of credit and in the making of investments. Equal rules also facilitate the task of consolidating companies in a financial group. The pure insurance risk (underwriting risks, etc.) of insurance companies is, however, as underlined in paragraph 7.1.1., subject to a separate solvency requirement. There are different requirements applicable to the insurance risk in life and non-life insurance companies. The separate capital requirement that covers underwriting risks, etc., will for insurance companies come in addition to the previously mentioned capital adequacy requirement applicable to both insurance companies and banks. The total statutory capital ratio is therefore for insurance companies the sum of the two separate requirements. The requirements do not create any problems with regard to the consolidation of, for example, Norwegian banks and insurance companies.

Allow me, at this point, to comment on Professor Van den Berghe's comparison between the actual capital of insurance companies and calculated solvency requirements for these companies, based on a combination of the rules in the EU directives which now apply to the measurement of capital in banks and insurance companies, cfr. paragraph 6.2.3. I disagree with such a comparison. If the requirements applicable to the asset side of banks are applied to insurance companies (i.e. if the EU rules for credit institutions are applied to insurance companies, as we do in Norway), one cannot at the same time use the existing EU solvency requirements for insurance companies. In such a situation, the EU provisions regarding solvency margin must be revised substantially, to the effect that the current 4% requirement must be reduced considerably, if not eliminated. The reason for this is that the EU (by using an indirect and approximate approach) implicitly has taken account of the credit risk on the asset side with the 4% requirement on the liability side.

Allow me to recall at this point that Norway, in keeping with the EEA Agreement, will convert to a two-track solvency requirement for insurance:

- The rules presented in paragraph 7.1 and paragraph 7.2.
- The EU directives on solvency margin.

With regard to this, I would like to mention that calculations show that once the Norwegian rules are satisfied, virtually all the EU solvency requirements will be satisfied. However, a formal introduction of the EU rules will ensure that the Norwegian requirements at any given time satisfy the EU requirements. It is in my opinion of the utmost importance to bear in mind that the current EU rules will entail a high degree of arbitrage due to the pronounced trend towards an increased integration and decompartmentalisation of financial institutions. The EU capital requirement of 4% on the liabilities side for insurance companies is implicitly the same as a 4% capital requirement on the asset side. This means that insurance companies' credits and investments have a risk weight of 50% compared to similar assets in banks' balance sheets. The implication of this will be a higher tendency towards intragroup arbitrage; insurance companies will take over a growing share of the credits and investments with the highest risk. More precisely: As a result of different capital requirements for banks and insurance companies, insurance companies will increasingly tend to grant credits and make investments which have a risk-weight of 100% for banks. With such an arbitrage of 100% risk-weighted credits and investments, the total capital requirement of a group will be substantially reduced. In the example I have chosen, the transfer to an insurance company of a loan with a risk weight of a 100% for a bank, will reduce the group's capital ratio associated with the asset in question with 50%. The current EU regulations (with completely different risk weighting of the assets of banks and insurance companies), will lead to a substantial rise in the risk of insurance companies within a group. This can only be avoided by establishing uniform rules.

The present EU rules will, furthermore, allow insurance companies to expand substantially without having to increase the core capital. The reason is that the EU directives now allow insurance companies to include subordinated loans as capital, as has been the case for banks in many years. Since insurance companies have little or no subordinated loans, they will be able to raise their level of subordinated loans as they expand.

This brings me to a more general comment concerning subordinated loans. In my opinion, the EU regulations should require that subordinated loans only be eligible for inclusion in supplementary capital (tier 2), if they can also be used to cover a loss if a bank (or insurance company) does not fail or is winded up. In Norway, for example, no share of subordinated loans was lost during the banking crisis. These loans remained a sound investment even during the height of the crisis experienced by the banks. This is because the loan contracts contained clauses which limited the use of subordinated loans to cover losses to only two situations: Bank failure or if a bank is taken under public administration for the purpose of being winded up. As you know, this was not the case in Norway. The troubled banks were bailed out by considerable capital infusion by the central government. In my view, one should allow subordinated loans to be used to cover losses immediately after the core capital has been lost, irrespective of whether the bank has failed, has been placed under public administration or continues as a going concern.

It is important to harmonise the definition of capital in banks and insurance companies, i.e. establish a common definition of which components qualify for inclusion in the capital base. Although definitions are better harmonised today than before the last revision of the different capital components which can be used to cover the solvency requirement of insurance companies, there are still some differences that should be adjusted.

One such difference is the rule which allows insurance companies to include undistributed reserves as part of the capital used to cover the solvency margin requirement. These reserves belong to the policyholders, although they are not formally distributed. This is not a major issue in Norway because virtually the entire surplus must be distributed among the individual contracts each year. It is my opinion that a large measure of risk is transferred to policyholders when life insurance companies are allowed to operate with substantial undistributed reserves, which can be used to satisfy the solvency margin requirement. The EU directives allow this, although the authorities in the individual member states may decide that such reserves cannot be included. As far as I know, Denmark has decided not to allow the inclusion of undistributed reserves. I feel it is important to disallow this possibility to include undistributed reserves in order to reduce the risk actually borne by the policyholders.

I would also like to mention that the USA has no federal regulatory framework which applies to the insurance sector. The NAIC has, however, provided model acts which more and more states are adopting. The NAIC has used the same principles that Norway has applied, but the formula for the total requirement is more complex. Likewise, higher risk-weights than in the EU directives are used for credit institutions. The NAIC has, for example, capital requirements which are based on risk weights between 0 and ca. 400 per cent (see paragraph 7.3).

By way of conclusion, I would like to point out that some people include market risk as a third risk factor to be considered in addition to credit and underwriting risk. I fully agree with this approach. It is possible to continue to work on the question of market risk, as the EU now does in relation to credit institutions, and incorporate this as an additional capital adequacy requirement at a later stage. However, this must not prevent the introduction of the best possible system today.

Certain discussants at the workshop have pointed out that the central banks supply banks with money, and that the banks themselves "create" money through their credit activity. In my opinion, this has little relevance in terms of which solvency requirement should be applied. It is a matter of monetary policy. It is also my opinion that the large liquidity risk facing banks does not constitute an argument in favour of differentiated rules. The banks' higher liquidity risk must be managed through necessary liquidity among the asset components, and this should not have any bearing on the solvency requirements. Furthermore, the central banks will act as lender of last resort in the event of a liquidity shortage.

Finally, it is my belief that different policyholders protection schemes should not be used as an argument in favour of different capital requirements. This is because a deposit insurance scheme relates to a situation where a disaster already is a fact.

7.3. **RISK-BASED CAPITAL IN THE UNITED STATES, DISCUSSION BY J. ROOS[4]**

7.3.1. INTRODUCTION

During the height of the banking industry solvency crisis (at the end of the eighties), the NAIC[5] began its considerations about the financial health of insurers. The NAIC adopted the "Solvency Policing Agenda for 1990". Six areas were defined for which more state regulation was necessary. One of those areas was the development of risk-based capital (RBC) requirements. The NAIC has adopted two new models, one for life/health insurers and one for property/casualty insurers. The model for life and health insurers became effective in 1993[6]. Only eight states yet adopted the model and its accompanying law. The model for property/casualty insurers has to take effect in 1995. For both branches the prescribed models have to be implemented by the beginning of 1997 for all states wishing to be certified through the NAIC's accreditation program[7].

7.3.2. RISK-BASED CAPITAL RATIO

The risk based capital ratio is defined as the percentage of actual surplus held by the insurer divided by the capital required by each individual risk-based capital component, adjusted for a covariance risk.

$$\frac{\text{actual surplus held by the insurer}}{\text{ACL RBC}} * 100\%$$

ACL RBC: authorized control level risk based capital

The calculation of this ratio is based on the annual statement of an insurer. The calculation of the ACL RBC will be described separately for life/health insurers and property/casualty insurers.
The total adjusted capital for both life/health insurers and property/casualty insurers consists of the capital, the surplus, the asset valuation reserve, the voluntary investment reserve and 50% of the dividend liability.

---

[4] Research-assistant at the Erasmus Finance & Insurance Centre.
[5] NAIC (National Association of Insurance Commissioners). The NAIC has no specific supervisory authority, but plays an important co-ordinating role in state regulation. The supervisory authority lays with the state regulator and the insurance department of the different states. However, the model statutes and regulations developed by the NAIC are often the reference basis by the state regulators and insurance departments.
[6] The Risk-Based Capital for life and/or health insurers model act.
[7] State insurance departments are accredited by the NAIC if they meet the NAIC's Financial Regulation Standards. These standards require that certain acts and regulations are adopted by a state and that some procedures are followed by that state. The insurance department also has to implement a certain organizational structure and a certain personnel policy.

7.3.3. THE ACL RBC OF LIFE INSURERS

The following risks are taken into account in the RBC ratio for life/health insurers:

- asset-default risk (C1)
- insurance risk (C2)
- interest-rate risk (C3)
- business risk (C4)

The formula to calculate the ACL RBC is[8]:

$$\text{ACL RBC} = \frac{\sqrt{(C1+C3)^2+(C2)^2+C4}}{2}$$

The risk-based capital is in general calculated by multiplying the value of relevant items from the annual statement and a RBC factor.

Asset-default risk is the risk of losses from bonds, mortgages, stocks, real estate and other investments through either default on payment of interest and/or principal or through loss of market value. The general calculation method for the risk-based capital will be modified with a size factor for the amount of bond issues (bond size factor) and a mortgage experience adjustment factor (MEA) for the different mortgages. The sum of the required capital for asset-default risk will also be adjusted with an asset concentration factor (the ten largest asset exposures up to a maximum of 30% require extra capital).

Insurance risk is the risk of mispricing products due to inappropriate assumptions and/or statistical fluctuations. When this happens the premium is unable to cover unfavorable changes in the mortality, morbidity, and expenses. The calculation of the required capital will be different for individual and group insurance. The required capital is determined by multiplying the difference between "life-insurance in-force" and "life insurance reserve" with a degressive factor (which reflects the decreasing risk for larger blocks of capital at risks).

The third risk, interest risk, can occur in a mismatched portfolio in periods of rising and falling interest rates. The general account annuity, deposit fund and life insurance reserves will be divided in three classifications: low-risk category, medium-risk category and high-risk category. Each risk category is given a certain RBC factor. The required capital is calculated by multiplying this RBC factor with the value of the above mentioned elements.

---

[8]   LOMA (1994): "Risk-Based Capital in the life insurance industry".

Not all the risks undertaken by a life insurer are covered by the first three risks (C1, C2, C3). The remaining risks will fall under the category of business risk. Examples of business risk are guarantee fund assessments, fraud and law suits. It is difficult to quantify business risk in a general way for all companies. The risk of guarantee fund assessment can be quantified by a percentage of the premium (e.g. 2% for life insurance and annuity insurance and 0,5% of the premium for health insurance).

An example of the calculation of risk-based capital for a life insurer is given in table 7.3.1. and 7.3.2. [9].

Table 7.3.1. a-e: Example of the basic NAIC RBC calculation for ABC Life Insurance Company

Table a. Basic NAIC RBC calculation for asset risk

Asset Risk (C-1)	Annual Statement Value (1)	RBC Factor (2)	MEA Factor (see table 2) (3)	Risk-Based Capital (1)*(2)*(3)
Bonds				
Class 1 Bonds (60 issuers)	$60,000,000	0.0030		$180,000
Class 2 Bonds (1 issuer)	2,000,000	0.0100		20,000
Bonds subject to Size Factor	62,000,000			200,000
Total number of Bond issuers	61			
Size Factor for Bonds (see table 2)				2.2836
Total RBC for Bonds				456,720
Commercial mortgages in Good Standing (6 loans)	12,000,000	0.0300	1700	612,000
Common Stock	2,000,000	0.3000		600,000
Real Estate (1 Property)	3,000,000	0.1000		300,000
Asset Concentration Factor (see Table 2)				680,000
Total asset risk (C-1)				**$2,648,720**

Table b. Basic NAIC RBC calculation for insurance risk

Insurance risk (C-2)	Annual Statement Value (1)	RBC Factor (2)	Risk-Based Capital (1)*(2)
Life insurance			
Individual Life Insurance			
Ordinary Life insurance In-Force = (a)	$600,000,000		
Life insurance Reserves = (b)	72,000,000		
Total Ordinary Life Insurance Net	528,000,000	see table 2	$778,000
Amount at Risk = (a) - (b)			
Total insurance risk (C-2)			**$778,000**

[9]   See Loma (1994).

Table c. Basic NAIC RBC calculation for interest rate risk

Interest Rate Risk (C-3)	Annual Statement Value (1)	RBC Factor (2)	Risk-Based Capital (1)*(2)
Life Insurance Reserves	$72,000,000	0.0075	$540,000
Annuity Reserves not Withdrawable (Low Risk)	1,000,000	0.0075	7,500
Annuity Reserves With Surrender Charge (medium Risk)	1,000,000	0.0150	15,000
Total interest risk (C-3)			**$562,500**

Table d. Basic NAIC RBC calculation for business risk

Business Risk (C-4)	Annual Statement Value (1)	RBC Factor (2)	Risk-Based Capital (1)*(2)
Life & Annuity Premiums	$5,000,000	0.0200	$100,000
Total Business Risk (C-4)			**$100,000**

Table e. Calculation for total risk based capital

Total Risk Based Capital	Risk-Based Capital
Total C-1	$2,648,720
Total C-2	778,000
Total C-3	562,500
Total C-4	100,000
Effect of Covariance	(685,099)
RBC Subtotal	3,404,121
Authorized Control Level RBC (ACLRBC) = 50% of RBC Subtotal	**$1,702,061**

Table 7.3.2. a-d: NAIC Life Risk-Based Capital Calculation for ABC Life Insurance Company (Backup Information to Basic RBC calculation)

Table a. Bond Size Factor

The size factor reflects additional modeling for different size portfolios which shows that the risk increases as the number of bond issuers decreases.

	# of issuers				Weighted issuers
First 50	50	*	2.5	=	125.0
Next 50	11	*	1.3	=	14.3
Total	60				139.3
Size Factor = Total Weighted Issuers/Total # of issuers					2.2836

Table b. Mortgage Experience Adjustment (MEA) Factor

The Mortgage Experience Adjustment (MEA) Factor is calculated for each company as the ratio for company ldelinquency experience to industry delinquency experience for the prior two years.

Table c. Asset Concentration Factor

The asset concentration factor reflects the additional risk of high concentrations in a single exposure by doubling the RBC factors of the 10 largest asset exposures up to a maximum of 30%.

Name of issuer	Type of Asset	$ amount		RBC Factor		Additional RBC
Company 1	Real Estate	3,000,000	*	0.10	=	$300,000
	Class 2 Bond	2,000,000	*	0.01	=	20,000
Company 2	Mortgage	2,000,000	*	0.03	=	60,000
Company 3	Mortgage	2,000,000	*	0.03	=	60,000
Company 4	Mortgage	2,000,000	*	0.03	=	60,000
Company 5	Mortgage	2,000,000	*	0.03	=	60,000
Company 6	Mortgage	2,000,000	*	0.03	=	60,000
Company 7	Mortgage	2,000,000	*	0.03	=	60,000
Total Asset Concentration Factor						$680,000

Table d. Life Insurance Risk (c-2)

RBC for Life Insurance - Factors for life insurance decrease as in-force business increases. This is to reflect the decrease in risk for larger blocks of life insurance.

Net amount at Risk			Factor		RBC
first 500 million	$500,000,000	*	0.0015	=	$750,000
next 4,500 million	28,000,000	*	0.0010	=	28,000
Total Net amount at Risk	$528,000,000				$778,000

7.3.4. THE ACL RBC OF PROPERTY/CASUALTY INSURERS

The general definition of the risk based capital ratio for property/casualty insurers is the same as for life insurers. The risks taken into account and the calculation of the ACL RBC are different. The risks are:

- asset risk
  * off-balance sheet risk (R0)
  * fixed income investment risk (R1)
  * equity investment risk (R2)
- credit risk (R3)
- loss reserve risk (R4)
- written premium risk (R5)

The formula to calculate the ACL RBC[10]:

$$ACL\ RBC = RO + \sqrt{(RI)^2 + (R2)^2 + (0,5*R3)^2 + [(0,5*R3) + R4]^2 + (R5)^2}$$

The sum of the required capital for the risk categories will be adjusted with a covariance factor. This reflects the thought that not all risk will appear at the same

[10]   ALBANESE, M.L. & MAYEWSKI, L.G. & McKENNA, M. (1994): " RBC: Beauty contest or non-event?", in Life/Health Best's Review, March 1994, pp. 33-36, 86-88.

time. However, this is not the case for off-balance sheet risk.

Most of the risks taken into account by the property/casualty insurers are not the same as those run by the life/health insurers. But capital is required for asset risk by both risk-based capital models. However, the risk-based capital charges for some assets differ.

The calculation of the required capital for asset risk is divided in three parts. The capital for off-balance sheet risk, the fixed income investment risk and the equity investment risk. The required capital is calculated by multiplying the statement value and the RBC factor.

The required capital for bonds is adjusted by a bond size factor. This capital for bonds is part of the capital that covers the fixed investment income risk. The required capital for the asset risk, except for the off-balance sheet risk will be adjusted for concentration risk (additional capital is needed for the 10 largest investment holdings up to a maximum of 30%).

To determine the required capital for credit risk a distinction is made between domestic and foreign affiliated and non-affiliated reinsurance.

The required capital to cover the loss reserve risk is generated by multiplying reserve leverage factors and the adjusted loss reserve. This has to be done for all distinct lines of business (18). There are adjustments for reserve concentration and reserve growth.

The last category of risk taken into account is the written premium risk. Almost the same method as far the loss reserve risk is used to generate the required capital for written premium risk. For the different lines of business the premium leverage factors must be multiplied by the adjusted written premium. There is an adjustment for premium growth and premium concentration.

Possible actions by the state regulator

The solvency margin is measured by the ratio of the actual solvency versus the required level (a RBC ratio of 100% is called Authorized Control Level (ACL)). Which action the state regulator will take for each of the different RBC levels is described in the table below.

RBC ratio (% of ACL)	RBC level	Response of state regulator
< 70%	Mandatory Control Level (MCL)	regulator must rehabilitate or liquidate the insurer
70% - <100%	Authorized Control Level (ACL)	insurer may be subjected to regulatory control
100% - <150%	Regulatory Action Level (RAL)	the regulator must examine and require corrective action of an insurer (confidential actions)
150% - <200%	Company Action Level (CAL)	the regulator must order an insurer to file a business plan. This plan is confidential
200% - <250%	Trend Test Corridor	- trend is negative: same action as by company action level - trend is not negative: no regulator response

7.4. DISCUSSION BY DRS. J.H. HOLSBOER[11]

7.4.1. CONSOLIDATED VERSUS SOLO-PLUS SUPERVISION

This issue of consolidated versus solo-plus supervision is very important. We strongly favour the solo-plus approach (separate supervision and specific additional measures where necessary to eliminate potential dangers when insurers and banks form conglomerates).

I think the Dutch situation with the so-called Protocol between the Insurance Supervisory Board and the Netherlands Central Bank can serve as a good example of adequate and pragmatic supervision of financial conglomerates.

We favour the solo-plus approach not only because of the unnecessary burden of consolidated supervision for insurers and the potential disrupting effects with regard to the level playing field, but also because of keeping a strict partition between the legal entities of the individual companies is in our opinion the best guarantee for the client/policyholder to prevent 'contagion'. Consolidation does not give the client any more guarantees: the legal responsibilities of the parent or holding company remain essentially the same, whether consolidated supervision is exercised or solo-plus supervision. Another case against consolidated supervision of conglomerates by the banking supervisor would be that in many countries (notable exceptions being Belgium, France and Germany) supervision of the banking industry is in the hands of the central bank which combines this task with its monetary duties, which could well lead to 'conflicts of interest' and 'political agendas' which should not intrude into objective supervisory procedures for insurance. Finally, supervision on a consolidated basis requires uniform solvency requirements for all parts of the financial conglomerate. As we know bank supervision is basically top down, material and pro-active, whereas our insurance supervision is much more bottom-up, normative and retro-active. The previous chapter clearly demonstrates that this combination of these approaches is well-nigh impossible.

7.4.2. DEVELOPMENT OF SUPERVISORY RULES IN RELATION TO 'INCIDENTS'

Discussions on the adequacy of supervisory rules are often triggered bij 'incidents' (like the S&L-banks in the US and BCCI in Europe). Perhaps this could also explain to some extent why Norway introduced BIS-rules in insurance supervision. But no matter what rules are in force, the role of the supervisory authorities (the way they use the information banks and insurers have to provide) is very crucial in preventing these incidents. All the information about financing of and investing in real estate projects did not prevent quite a number of companies from getting into trouble.

---

[11] Member of the Executive Board of ING, the Netherlands.

7.4.3. APPLYING THE BIS-RATIO TO INSURANCE COMPANIES

In my opinion, applying the BIS-rules to insurance companies (as is done in Norway) is artificial, unnecessary and potentially distracting.

Artificial, because you just can't apply the BIS-rules to insurance companies. These rules are tailor-made for banks. This is demonstrated for the case of the revaluation reserves (see paragraph 7.4.4). Moreover lower, less prudent, insurance reserves would lead to lower solvency requirements, without a compensatory formula as provided for under the insurance rules (based upon claims-experience). Unnecessary, because there is a much more adequate way of dealing with asset risks of insurance companies: the 'risk-based capital' solvency regulations adopted in the US, which cater precisely for this risk (see paragraph 7.4.5).
Potentially distracting, because it fails to appreciate the significance of the insurance liabilities as potential risk factors. Contrary to the suggestion that this mainly regards the non-life sector, it is also the case for life insurance companies. Take for instance the longevity risk, which forced us to make very substantial provisions. Life insurance is in fact a sort of long-term open-end contract. An extra life-expectancy of 5 years would mean serious problems for insurers of annuities!

7.4.4. REVALUATION RESERVES OF INSURANCE COMPANIES AS TIER 2 CAPITAL

Revaluation reserves of insurance companies are fundamentally different from revaluation reserves of banks, because of the longer term nature of their investments and the nature of the investments themselves (banks hardly invest in equities or property). Whether capital gains are realized (and funds accumulate as tier 1 capital) or not (and funds are put in the revaluation reserves) is not really fundamental with regard to the solvency of insurance companies.
A large part of the revaluation reserves should therefore be considered as free reserves. This would also prevent the rather 'peculiar' situation of the large life insurance company in the simulation sample (see chapter 6) (which incidentally is NN Life), for which a large part of the revaluation reserves could not be included as solvency funds (because, for purposes of the BIS-ratio, tier 2 capital can never exceed the tier 1 capital).
This does not mean that there should not be some provision for events like e.g. a stock market crash. Within NN we maintain for that purpose a 40% 'buffer' of the actual stock market value (30% for real estate) on top of our internal solvency requirements, which are already significantly higher than the legal solvency margins. Therefore, you could say that we have a 'BIS-ratio' of 40% (for the stock portfolio), even when our portfolio is essentially low-risk! So, here we have a further reason for treating this revaluation reserve as tier 1 capital.

7.4.5. RISK BASED CAPITAL SOLVENCY REGULATIONS

It is also interesting to look at 'risk based capital' (RBC) approach, which has recently been developed for insurance companies in the US, Canada (already in force) and Australia (in force as from 30/9/95) (see also paragraph 7.3). The RBC-approach addresses just the problems we are discussing now. It is a method to determine the minimally required solvency in relation to volume and risk profile. Contrary to present European solvency regulations the RBC-approach does take into account a number of relevant financial (non-insurance) risks. According to the risk profile solvency-requirements are set for different components of investments, premiums and provisions.

For life insurers one takes into account asset risks (investment risks, incl. reinsurance risks), insurance risks (mortality and morbidity risk), interest rate risks (incl. mismatch) and the normal business and management risks.

For Property & Casualty insurers underwriting risks (based on provisions and written premiums), investment risks and credit risks (incl. reinsurance risks) and normal business and management risks are taken into account.

Already there has been a notable effect on behaviour of insurers in North America:

- in general we perceive a 'flight to quality' by intermediaries and customers;
- a more risk-averse and less growth-oriented behaviour by insurers, also with regard to investments;
- more hedging of market risks and transfer of risks to the capital market by securitization;
- a stronger tendency to raise premiums for high-risk activities;
- development of products which shift the investment risk to the client;
- improvement of balance sheet ratios (and sometimes ratings);
- increasing tension between required solvency and competitive strength (pricing of products).

A fundamental problem of course is whether or not such 'evasive' behaviour could lead to inefficient market structures.

7.4.6. ROLE OF RATING AGENCIES

There is no mention in the workshop papers of the possible role of rating agents with regard to supervision. It is stated, that the development of unit linked products 'diverts' the investment risk to the client. Therefore less solvency would be required from the point of view of supervision. As it turns out, for instance in the US, in that situation 'the market' (by means of rating agencies) imposes 'commercial' solvency requirements on insurance companies in order for them to be able to sell those products. The question is therefore, whether or not legal supervision should only be 'supplementary' to market supervision. Legal supervision could then be geared to those situations which market supervision can not solve (e.g. maintaining the integrity of the financial system).

7.5. DISCUSSION BY DR. K.W. KNAUTH[12]

7.5.1. SOLVENCY REGULATIONS FOR FINANCIAL CONGLOMERATES

The analysis carried out by the Erasmus Finance & Insurance Centre clearly points out the differences which exist between the risk protection scheme applied by banks and that applied by insurance companies.

However, I would like to make a few additional remarks on the question whether, as far as holdings between banks and insurance companies are concerned, there are specific risks which make it necessary to harmonize the own funds regulations for insurance companies and banks and subsequently to introduce consolidation. I deny any such necessity.

The main arguments put forward by the advocates of consolidation of companies in a financial conglomerate are the risk of contagion and "double gearing", i.e. multiple use of own funds.

7.5.2. THE RISK OF CONTAGION

Normally, there can only be a risk of contagion if an insurance company is obliged by legal ties to assume a liability for losses of a company in which it holds a participating interest. However, losses of share values are not a liability problem but must be considered a normal investment risk. The risk of a loss of value is inherent in any investment. With regard to insurance companies, the investment principles of spread and diversification ensure that the insurance company is not exposed to any real danger despite such a loss. Also, a loss may at any time be limited by selling the interest at the stock exchange. Moreover, the principle of security of investments obliges insurance companies to invest in companies where insolvency and consequently complete loss of value are almost impossible. This is one of the principal reasons for the fact that insurance companies acquire minority holdings in banks, whose operations are subject to strict state supervision. Therefore, it would seem paradoxical if, from the regulatory point of view, the secure investment in a credit institution was considered more risky than a holding in an industrial company.

---

[12] Gesamtverband der Deutchen Versicherungswirtschaft e.V., Germany.

7.5.3. DOUBLE GEARING

In the case of a unilateral or cross holding between an insurance company and a credit institution there is just as little cumulation of risks as in the case of a holding of an insurance company in an industrial company. The idea of a cumulation of risks in the form of "double gearing" obviously originates from reflections of the banking supervisors which are to a certain extent justified for holdings between one bank and another. For banks the credit risk is the dominating risk. It depends on economic factors and usually affects all the credit institutions in a banking group simultaneously. Thus, the investment risk and the commercial risk are correlated. This also causes a decrease in the value of the bank holding. Thus, the bank is not able to cover its own losses in its credit business by selling its shares in a bank. Losses in the credit business and losses of share value put a double burden on the bank. Moreover, the risk within a banking group is aggravated by the phenomenon of a "run to banks".

However, this doubling effect with regard to risks does not occur in the case of a holding between a bank and an insurance company. The business risk of a property or a life insurer is not correlated with the risk of a bank holding. On the contrary, high insurance claims may be paid by selling bank shares, and a bank may cover losses in its banking business by disposing of its shares in insurance companies. An insurance company is not exposed to the risk of a "run to banks", either, because it does not accept short-term deposits. Therefore, there is no reason at all to treat holdings between banks and insurance companies in a different way than their holdings in non-supervised companies.

The possibility to use the own funds several times does not seem correct, either, because insurance companies do not specifically finance holdings e.g. in banks from their own funds but from all their assets. This means that both their own funds and their committed assets, which serve to represent their technical provisions, are used to finance holdings. However, this already invalidates the assumption for applying "double gearing". Actually, this discussion is characterized by the ideas of banking supervision, as well, which are applied in this respect to a situation which is not comparable to insurance.

7.5.4. RESEARCH INTO THE POSSIBILITY OF A GLOBAL APPROACH FOR THE CALCULATION OF THE SOLVENCY REQUIREMENTS OF FINANCIAL CONGLOMERATES

I agree to the analysis carried out in chapter 6. Its knowledge of the insurance business has led to results which will undoubtedly surprise many banker. As a representative of the interests of insurance I am glad about this.

That is why I restrict myself to a few short remarks:

-   The analysis states that the question has never been raised whether credit
    institutions should also take insurance technical risks into account. According
    to it, this is due to the fact that banks are not engaged in insurance operations.
    However, in this respect, I would like to raise the question whether the
    guarantee business of the banks and the use of derivative financial instruments
    for hedging purposes may not be considered a form of insurance business.
-   It is considered whether, when calculating the minimum solvency, the ex-
    change risk within the EU should be taken into account. The corrections which
    this would require are impressive. Nevertheless, it does not seem absolutely
    necessary to do so:
    *   Unlike the banking business, which has meanwhile become very interna-
        tional, the insurance business continues to be national. Even the opening of
        the Single Market will, in my opinion, not lead to a noticeable development
        of a European business during the next few years.
    *   In 1999 at the latest, the Economic and Monetary Union with a unique
        European currency is to be implemented. After this date, there will no
        longer be any exchange risk even in the European market.
    *   The Third Insurance Directives require that only 20 % of the investments
        may be in assets which are not matching assets. Thus, the exchange risk is
        limited accordingly.
-   On the part of the banks, it is sometimes suggested that, for reasons of
    competition, the insurance companies should adopt the solvency rules applying
    to banks. This demand has to be contradicted:
    *   The function of supervisory legislation is the protection of the clients of
        banks and insurance companies. Because of the importance of the banks for
        the capital market, in banking supervision the protection of companies has
        the same priority.
    *   Insurance companies and banks use different methods to fulfil this supervi-
        sory purpose. The analysis carried out by the Erasmus Finance & Insurance
        Centre has shown in an impressive way that the insurance companies have
        a varied precaution scheme which is very much designed according to their
        type of business. In this scheme own funds play only a minor role. As
        opposed to this, the only risk prevention measure applied by credit institu-
        tions is the securing of their banking business on a pro rata basis by their
        own funds (8 %).
    *   The efficiency of both supervisory systems may only be judged by asking
        whether they fulfil the tasks which have been assigned to them. If the
        frequency of bankruptcies is taken as a criterion, the risk protection scheme
        of the insurance companies will clearly be the winner of this test. Therefore,
        aspects of competition should not lead to the replacement of an insurance
        system which fulfils the supervisory purposes by a more doubtful and also

more expensive banking supervisory system. The deposit-guarantee schemes of the banks clearly show that the banking supervisors doubt the adequacy of their own system.

* Until now, no proof has been furnished of the alleged distortion of competition to the disadvantage of the banks. It is not acceptable only to compare the investment business of the insurance companies to the banking operations. On the part of the banks it is not taken into account in this respect that the investment principles compel the insurance companies to pursue a business policy which is very different from that of the banks. A number of highly-profitable financial operations (syndicate operations, securities transactions, arbitrage transactions, etc.) as well as borrowing are denied to insurance companies. All kinds of profitable investments are restricted by spreading and diversification principles. These differences should first of all be quantified. It is only after this has been done that it can be decided whether there is any discrimination with regard to competition caused by supervisory legislation and who is put at a disadvantage by it.

7.6. DISCUSSION BY P. PEARSON[13]

7.6.1. SOLVENCY REGULATIONS FOR FINANCIAL CONGLOMERATES

The EC solvency requirements for insurance undertakings date back to 1974 for non-life insurance and to 1979 for life assurance. Recently interest has grown in examining a possible need to 'update' these requirements. Are they up-to-date with developments in the financial sector; are they still adequate to take account of the relevant risks incurred by insurers; are there any lessons to be learnt from recent solvency rules for credit institutions, extending to off-balance sheet items also; what are the merits of solvency requirements developed elsewhere, such as the USA ('Risk Based Capital'), Canada, or Norway?

EC insurance supervisors are aware of these questions. Indeed, the Third Non-Life Insurance Directive 92/49/EEC and the Third Life Assurance Directive 92/96/EEC require the European Commission to table a report before 1 July 1997 on the possible need to modify the solvency margin requirements.

The reason for this dates back to the negotiations on the Third Directives. The Commission had proposed to introduce measures preventing the double gearing of capital in insurance groups. In a broader sense, this issue had been raised in the discussions on financial conglomerates in Brussels. A longer term view was preferred by the Member States. Hence the general obligation, going beyond double gearing, to look at the entire solvency margin requirements.

---

[13] DG XV, European Commission.

One specific point, albeit unrelated point to the above, which was raised in Chapter 5, merits attention. The philosophy behind solvency regulations in the banking and insurance sectors refers to the existence of 'extra buffers'. It is stated that:

- the banking sector relies on deposit guarantee schemes, while
- the insurance sector relies more on extra supervision and stricter reserving rules.

Is this statement accurate, as the existence of deposit guarantee schemes in banking has more to do with 'life after death', i.e. after the failure of a credit institution, than with the supervision on a going concern basis. The statement that banking supervision relies on the existence of these schemes would however seem to go too far. There is of course an incidence in that deposit guarantees, acting as a safety net, may help prevent a run on a bank in that a degree of comfort is offered to clients that (a portion of) their monies will not be lost. From this perspective, the prudential problems of contagion risk and systemic risk are taken into account. (In the UK a similar scheme in the life assurance sector exists: the policyholder protection fund).

Furthermore, it is not clear of which elements the 'extra supervision' in the insurance sector would be composed. The term 'extra' implies something going beyond that in the banking sector. The contrary may in fact be argued, leaving aside the obvious differences in supervisory rules where banking and insurance business diverge, banking regulation may in fact be argued to go beyond that in insurance - at least as far as EC legislation is concerned. This could be argued in the case of for instance the treatment of exposures to large clients, the supervision of groups, the definitions of capital to support business or the treatment of new financial instruments. A point in fact are the recent changes to the definition of own funds for insurance companies in the Third Insurance Directives, incorporating elements (subordinated loan capital, perpetuals) that had been introduced in the banking Own Funds Directive 89/299/EEC at an earlier stage.

7.6.2. MINIMUM GUARANTEE FUNDS

An interesting point of comparison between the banking and insurance rules concerns the minimum solvency margins and guarantee funds for insurance under-takings. The First Non-Life Directive and the First Life Directive define the guarantee funds as one third of the minimum solvency margin. Depending on the class of business being carried out, the guarantee funds may not drop below certain minima. For non-life insurance, the amounts were fixed in 1973 (except for credit insurance, which was established in 1987), for life assurance the relevant amounts were fixed in 1979. None of these amounts have been amended since those dates, in spite of the fact that there exists an obligation to carry out a regular review every

5 years of these amounts at least in the non-life sector (see Article 3 of Directive 76/580/EEC, amending the First Non-Life Directive, later amended by the Second Non-Life Directive). Such reviews have never occurred in practice.

The minimum solvency margin thresholds are ECU 10 million (and ECU 7 million) for non-life insurance (Art. 16(3) First Non-Life Directive), and ECU 10 million for life assurance (Art. 19(1)b First Life Directive). Appendix 7.A. shows an evolution of these amounts based on the consumer price index as a rough basis of comparison. The increase for non-life would be to ECU 50 and 35 million (from ECU 10 and 7 million respectively). For life insurance the amount would increase from ECU 10 million to ECU 25 million. (By way of example, on the basis of these figures the minimum solvency margin requirement of a non-life company with a ECU 50 million premium base would increase from ECU 8.2 million to ECU 9 million).

An update of the minimum guarantee funds on the same basis (consumer price index, see Appendix 7.1) indicates that the amounts in life and non-life would result close to ECU 2 million (with a slightly higher figure for credit insurance).

It is of interest for the present discussion to see that if similar updates are carried out for the minimum start up capital of ECU 5 million for credit institutions under the Second Banking Directive 89/646/EEC, that figure would now be ECU 6 million. One third of that figure corresponds to the updated minimum guarantee fund requirements for insurers of ECU 2 million.

Appendix 7.A.

Thresholds and minimum guarantee funds

Insurance undertakings - updating

	Consumer price index EUR 12	Increase until end 1993
1973 first non-life	29,2	382,2%
1979 first life	57,5	144,9%
1983 credit insurance	88,0	60,0%
1989 second bank directive	116,3	21,1%
1993 end year index	140,8	

Thresholds

	Present value ecu	Updated value ecu	Updated rounded value ecu
Non-life	7.000.000	33.753.425	35.000.000
(article 16.3)	10.000.000	48.219.178	50.000.000
Life			
(article 19)	10.000.000	24.486.957	25.000.000

Guarantee funds[14]

	Present min.funds ecu	Updated min.funds ecu	Updated rounded figures ecu
Non-life	400.000	1.928.767	2.000.000
(article 17)	300.000	1.446.575	1.500.000
	200.000	964.384	1.000.000
(credit insurance)	1.400.000	2.240.000	2.250.000
Life	800.000	1.958.957	2.000.000
(article 20)	600.000	1.469.217	1.500.000
	500.000	1.224.348	1.250.000
	100.000	244.870	250.000

Credit institutions[15]

	Present min.funds ecu	Updated min.funds ecu	Updated rounded figures ecu
start capital	5.000.000	6.053.310	6.000.000

[14]   There is a difference with the results in appendix 6.C. This difference is a result of the sources used to calculate the average consumer price index.

[15]   See footnote 8.

8. Why financial conglomerates?

Strategic Issues

L.A.A. Van den Berghe
Erasmus Finance& Insurance Centre (NL)
De Vlerick School voor Management (B)

8.1. WHAT IS THE REASONING BEHIND THE FORMATION OF A FINANCIAL CONGLOMERATE ?

According to a recent study for the OECD, Koguchi (1993) concluded that "financial conglomeration can be viewed as an inevitable adaptation to the changing financial environment".

All enterprises involved in the establishment of a financial conglomerate state that their decisions have been based on the potential synergies between their respective core businesses. Exploiting these synergies could enhance their competitive position and procure them the necessary competitive edge in the tough competitive battle.

The synergies can potentially be found into two directions:

- economies of scale: through an increase in the turnover without a proportional increase in the costs, the average costs decrease (to a considerable extent); the higher the fixed costs a company is working with, the better the perspectives for economies of scale; in a mature market environment it is not always possible to reach the most optimal volume of business; in this case economies of scope can become the substitute[1];
- economies of scope: in our opinion it is possible to distinguish between three potential sources of economies of scope:
  * the most common source of economies of scope lies in the "cost"-effect; such a cost-effect arises if two or more products can be jointly produced at

---

[1] For more details see e.g. Dickinson & Dinensis (1993).

a lower cost than if produced separately. This sharing of inputs will only be possible if factors of production are not fully employed because otherwise "congestion" would be occurring;

* besides this "cost"-effect of economies of scope, also "value"-effects can be observed: complimentarities between products or services demanded can lower the information cost for the consumer and can (eventually) increase the value (better co-ordination, more tailored, etc.);

* a third source of economies of scope can be found in a better risk spreading: in case of (partially) offsetting risks, diversification can lead to a reduction of the business risk and a reduction of the variability of cash flows (e.g. fee income decreases the dependence of banks upon interest rate fluctuations).

So, through the combined use of funds, technology, know how, distribution outlets, etc., it is possible to arrive at lower costs, to perform better or/and to deliver a better service; the better the complimentarity between activities, products, service systems, etc., the higher the chances for economies of scope.

Since both types of "economies" will interfere in practice, it is better to look more closely at the potential types of synergies between banks, insurance companies and investment services. Potentials for synergies can be found in the manufacturing of the services, in the back-office, the administration as well as in the front office and from the client's perspective. Some examples in this respect:

- transfer of know how, combined staff and R&D;
- combined Asset Liability Management;
- combination of expertise on the level of investment advice;
- new distribution outlets for cross selling and for "all-round financial plan-ning"-advice;
- combination of the marketing efforts (e.g. communication expenses such as advertising, client relations);
- diversification of risk, more stable income and dividends;
- pooling of investments in and use of technology.

8.2. FINANCIAL CONGLOMERATES: NEW WAVE STRATEGIC THINKING?[2]

We want to develop the thesis that the formation of certain types of financial conglomerates can be seen as an application of the new strategic thinking of "stretch and leverage".

Before establishing this thesis in greater detail a short summary of the classical and modern view on strategic thinking is necessary.

---

[2]   Based on Van den Berghe [1994a].

8.3. STRATEGY AT THE LIMITS OF THE POSSIBLE: THE MANAGEMENT RECIPE OF THE NINETIES

For decennia, the management literature stressed the need to have a business strategy. The rapid changing economic environment with the European unification, the liberalisation of the world trade, the globalisation of the financial world, etc. were all factors that convinced most of the enterprises of the need of such a strategy. The raplex environment with the heavy competition does not allow any more to live upon past market success and historical experiences.

The traditional recipe to set up a business strategy can be summarised as follows[3]:

- step 1: state the mission of your company and the goals you want to achieve in the long and short term;
- step 2: analyse thoroughly the external environment and try to detect opportunities and threats (O&T)
- step 3: analyse thoroughly your internal environment and try to detect the strengths and weaknesses (S&W);
- step 4: confront your ambitions (step 1) with your possibilities (step 3) and with the specific external threats and opportunities (step 2) in order to make a choice between the alternative strategies you could follow.

This choice will be dictated by your own strengths and weaknesses and by the boundaries set through the external threats and opportunities. The classical recipe[4] is that the best strategies look for an optimal fit between ambitions and the SWOT-analysis (steps 2 and 3).

This classical view has been recently attacked by Hamel & Prahalad (1993). These new management gurus proclaim that enterprises, who want to excel and to build a lasting competitive advantage, must be very ambitious in their strategic choices and must not restrict their choice by internal limitations. It is not the optimal fit between possibilities and goals that counts. On the contrary, ambitious strategic intentions stimulate creativity and invention. It is not the strategic fit but the strategic gap that leads to a less stifled environment and to "outward bounding" of hindrances.

In fact the Schumpeterian entrepreneur is back in the picture as the central force to build upon "core competence".
In our opinion it is wrong to believe that these new ideas make the classic recipe useless. On the contrary both ideas are complimentary to a large extent. The

---

[3]   For more details see Van den Berghe & De Waal (1988).
[4]   The godfathers of these views are Ansoff (1965), Chandler (1962), and Porter (1991).

classical strategic prescriptions focus more on analysis and implementation techniques, while the new ideas are more concentrated on the strategic thinking process and the entrepreneurial philosophy that directs the strategic intentions and choices.

This new wave of management thinking can be used perfectly to explain the formation of financial conglomerates. Nevertheless it needs to be broadened first to incorporate also the external boundaries.

8.4. STRATEGY AT THE LIMITS OF THE POSSIBLE GOES FURTHER THAN INTERNAL CREATIVITY

The hypothesis that managers should not limit their ambition and creativity too much by internal restrictions applies also to the external restrictions. Strategic ambitions can lead to a blurring of the boundaries set by external rules, consumer attitudes etc.

Although external boundaries can be tough to overcome in the short term, they are certainly more flexible and adaptable in the long run. Two examples to prove this statement:

-   The regulatory environment can be restrictive and even prohibitive. Nevertheless regulation and deregulation are phenomena that show a certain pendulum movement. The forces behind that pendulum live in the society: the politicians, their voters, the consumers, the interest groups etc. Also enterprises are members in this process.
-   The consumers play a key role in the success of marketing strategies. Nevertheless market research[5] shows clearly that attitudes and behaviour of consumers are the product of individual as well as societal forces. The suppliers can exercise quite a great influence on these attitudes and behaviour. This is daily proven by some concrete examples.
    The mere existence of advertising shows that consumers can be "educated". Also the market behaviour of free riders can influence the consumers demand in such a respect that the market equilibrium can even be under attack. Illustrative in this respect is the penetration strategy of foreign banks and insurance companies that changed the market landscape in several European countries to a considerable degree.

Consequently we do believe that ambitious entrepreneurs with inventive and creative strategies, that go beyond the classical solutions, can be at the origin of important changes in the economic environment. If these strategies add value to

---

[5]   This has been proved clearly in a market research done by De Vlerick School voor Management of the University of Ghent (see Van den Berghe (1989 and 1993) & Verweire (1993)).

their stakeholders (internal value, external economies, higher quality, etc.) it becomes clear that, in a free market economy and a democratic system, they will also stimulate important changes in the external environment (demand structures, market regulation, supervisory rules, etc.).

8.5. THE FORMATION OF FINANCIAL CONGLOMERATES CAN BE A STRATEGY AT THE LIMITS OF THE POSSIBLE

This statement will be supported by two concrete examples of financial conglomerations. One is more oriented towards the internal restrictions, the other to the external limitations.

8.5.1. INTERNAL CREATIVITY AT THE LIMITS OF THE POSSIBLE

The FORTIS case is a good proof of the accelerator and multiplicator-effect of the strategic gap between ambitions and internal possibilities.

This financial conglomerate has been built up in 1990 through an alliance between the Belgian AG-group and the Dutch AMEV-VSB group. This last group was itself the product of a merger between an insurer (AMEV) and a savings bank (VSB). The AG-group was mainly an insurer, who had acquired through the years two smaller banks (Metropolitan Bank and Tiense Bank).

Before their alliance, both groups were pictured as potential acquisition candidates, because they would become too small to play a true international role, and too large to stick to a pure local niche strategy. Their "stuck in the middle" position made them vulnerable, but at the same time it was at the origin of their ambitious plans. Their alliance not only decreased their vulnerability but at the same time it was the engine that started an incredible process of internationalisation and diversification. The managers of the Fortis concern gave evidence of an ambitious strategic intention that was far greater than their original internal possibilities ever would have suggested.

Some concrete examples in this respect:

-   before their alliance, the consolidated own funds of AG were estimated at 24 billion BEF; those of the AMEV/VSB group at some 78 billion BEF. At the end of 1993 their consolidated own funds were estimated at more than 160 billion BEF.
-   in 1991 they acquired the group division of the American insurer "Mutual Benefit Life" for the price of around 15 billion BEF;
-   in 1992 they agreed upon an alliance with the Spanish bank "la Caixa" and got a 40% stake in Spain's largest life insurer VidaCaixa, a 60% stake in the non-life insurer SegurCaixa and a 50% stake in the sales organization AgenCaixa, for a price of some 7 billion BEF;

- in the meantime the Dutch bank branch acquired leasing company TOPLease and extended its banking network by the addition of a number of savings banks. The insurance arm bought several insurance portfolio's, reached a commercial agreement with one of the largest Dutch health insurers (VGZ);
- in 1993 the Fortis group achieved a major step forward by acquiring control of the largest Belgian savings bank and its sister insurance company; although the final price for their actual 49,9% is not yet defined, it will be close to 35 billion BEF;
- consolidated own funds at the end of 1995: > 340 billion BEF.

8.5.2. EXTERNAL (AND INTERNAL) CREATIVITY AT THE LIMITS OF THE POSSIBLE

As pointed out before, financial conglomerates are mainly established to realise the potential synergies between banking, insurance and investment services. Those potential economies are even the arguments used by supervisory authorities to deregulate their strict limitations and to allow this type of conglomerations.

The economic literature has not yet been able to clearly prove the existence of important economies of scale and scope in the financial sector (Forestieri - 1993). The enterprises involved in the formation of financial conglomerates are built too recently to have already sufficient quantitative evidence of important economies. Recent research of Coopers & Lybrand (1993) shows clearly that the advantages will be far higher and the possibilities far greater if the co-operation leads to further integration. Recent market research of ours[6] has also shown that an integrated client approach in the direction of "all finance" can be a competitive advantage for certain types of clients.

The problem with the integration between banks, insurance companies and investment services is that the regulatory environment does not allow this and that moreover the traditional marketing approaches are different and to some extent even incompatible with each other.

Confronted with this gap between opportunities and possibilities an entrepreneur needs ambitious creativity to develop a real integration strategy. A good case in this respect is ING-Group.

The ING-Group has been formed through the merger of an insurance group (Nationale-Nederlanden) and a banking group (NMB-Postbank group, itself a merger between the NMB bank and the state-owned Postbank). The top management was convinced that the full rewards of this merger could only be achieved through a structure that facilitates the maximum co-operation between banking, insurance and investment activities. They did not want to orient this new structure

---

[6]   See e.g. Van den Berghe, L. (1989) & (1993) and Verweire, K. (1993).

towards the regulatory prescriptions or the historical boundaries between the economic sectors. Nor did they agree to base their operational strategy upon the legal structure of the group-enterprises. Their main ambition was to structure the group in accordance with the strategy to form an "all finance group" and to base this structure fundamentally upon the market forces and the new management ideas of being "mean & lean" (Holsboer - 1993).

The new structure has been implemented at the beginning of 1994 and is for the Dutch market primarily based on the market segmentation prevailing at the "distribution"-level. The group will reorganise all activities around the different types of distribution channels they use to reach their clients (banking branches, agency systems, independent insurance intermediaries and direct selling through the Postbank). Within those distribution pillars an integration will be aimed at between banking, insurance and investment services. For each type of distribution a corresponding marketing mix will be developed (products, communication, prices). This integration can be rewarding but is not without risks. All market segments can not be served through the same type of distribution approach. A mature market is characterised by diversification on the level of client needs and products offered, as well as on the level of distribution approaches. Therefore, a "multi-channel" approach offers the advantage of a broader market coverage. Nevertheless hybrid marketing systems can also induce the risk of cannibalisation. It is therefore of the utmost importance to optimise the value added by each distribution system and to reach an equilibrium between those different types of distribution.

Due to the existing legal "specialisation requirements" set by the supervisory authorities, this operational integration will have to be backed by the traditional different legal entities for banking, life insurance, non-life insurance, investment services, etc.

In our opinion, the steps taken by the ING-management not only prove to be innovative and market driven, but moreover they show a good dose of ambition to develop a strategy that goes further than the strategic fit into the direction of "stretch and leverage". If this strategic gap will prove to have the boomerang-effect that is predicted in the literature, remains to be seen; one must not forget to mention some of the potential risks involved in the new management recipe.

8.6.   CONCLUSIONS

The formation of a financial conglomerate may be perfectly in accordance with the new management ideas on inventive and ambitious strategic thinking. Nevertheless this line of thinking is not without danger. Conscious risk taking is at the very heart of every entrepreneurship, but it is clear that an underestimation of risks involved or an insufficient attention towards risk evaluation can be fatal for any economic initiative.

The more innovative and creative a manager is, the higher the risks involved will be. This is not only true for R&D, the entrance of a new market or the marketing of a complete new product, but holds also for the establishment of a joint venture or the integration of activities or enterprises.

The Schumpeterian entrepreneurship is crucial for any economic progress. Nevertheless, the recipe of ambition and invention can lead to quite a number of defensive and even aggressive reactions. The resistance against changes, the fear for one's own position, etc. are well-known but at the same time dangerous phenomena.

Stressing the central role of the top management for the creative and ambitious use of the core competence may not lead to ignoring the importance of the total support and co-operation of everybody within the organisation. This is certainly the case in a "people's business" such as the financial service sector. It is important in this respect to remember that the chain is as strong as it's weakest link.

The new management recipe is an important upgrading of the classical strategic thinking but is not the sole solution to the successful implementation of a business strategy. The classical "tools" will still play an important role in the implementation of the strategic intentions developed on the base of the new insights.

In our opinion, the formation of financial conglomerates is not a temporary fashion but more a structural phenomenon. The underlying diversification strategy is supported by supply as well as market driven forces. The most ambitious strategies answer to the most modern management recipes.

Nevertheless the potential risks involved alarm the supervisory authorities. It can be foreseen that new regulations will come up to cope with these potential risks. It will therefore be necessary that objective and detailed examinations are made of the underlying economies of financial conglomerates, not only for the enterprises involved, but for the society at large. If these hard facts will not be forwarded in the future, it could be that even with innovative and ambitious management the strategic gap will prove to be far too large to be bridged.

9. Summary and Conclusions

L.A.A. Van den Berghe
A. Oosenbrug
K. Verweire
Erasmus Finance& Insurance Centre

9.1. PART I - DEFINITIONS

Although the formation of financial conglomerates has attracted a great deal of attention, one of the great difficulties is the demarcation of what institutions can be considered to be "financial conglomerates". There are different definitions according to the different purposes they serve.

Although not everybody agrees that there is a real need for a clear and general definition, the mere fact that stricter regulation will probably be developed for those diversified groups makes it obvious that the lack of such a definition can lead to considerable distortions in the "level playing field" between diversified and more or less specialised firms. This difference can also lead to "regulatory arbitrage".

The first part of this study is therefore devoted to a detailed analysis of the different definitions in order to come up with one global definition or at least a global framework for defining financial conglomerates.

9.1.1. WHAT ARE THE ESSENTIAL ELEMENTS THAT CONSTITUTE A FINANCIAL CONGLOMERATE ?

Owing to the bad connotations which are linked to the word "conglomerate", some specialists prefer the word "group" rather than "conglomerate". We think that the adjective "financial" may already point out that it is not a conglomerate in the normal sense of the word. Therefore, we have no objection against the term "financial conglomerate" and we even prefer it to a "financial group": a financial group can also mean a group of financial institutions of the same kind while this is certainly not the case with the term "financial conglomerate".

The relevant components concerning the definition of a financial conglomerate (and prevailing in most definitions) are that:

- it relates to a group of enterprises, and
- it's a combination of different kinds of financial institutions; this can be translated to the concept of being subject to different types of supervisory rules. The fact that we talk about financial institutions means already that there exists some complementarity between the different products.

These 2 points are examined somewhat more in detail.

9.1.2. DEFINING A GROUP OF ENTERPRISES

The biggest problem in defining a financial conglomerate is the definition of the concept "group". From the Norwegian case, analysed by S. Simonsen (Banking, Insurance and Securities Commisssion, Norway), it is clear that their straightforward regulation causes less problems in defining the "group" concept.
The definition of a group is also a very delicate issue because of the supervisory consequences. P. Pearson of the European Commission (DG XV) expresses it as follows: "The definition of the financial conglomerate must describe the "group" of undertakings to which certain supervisory rules should be applied".

In theory, not legal prescriptions but economic optimisation should decide what structure is best suited to set up a financial conglomerate[1]. This problem was also recognized by the European Commission when they worked out a definition of the "périmètre de la consolidation", but finally (after a 7 year discussion) the European Commission has opted for a legal definition.
Perhaps it's better to look at three cases to examine this problem more deeply.

First, consider a number of financial institutions linked through majority holdings. In the first chapter, we have defined majority holdings as participations of more than 50 per cent ("mother/daughter" relationship).
If these companies provide different financial services (see the next point), no problem exists: such a group can be defined as a financial conglomerate. This also corresponds to the opinion of the specialists whose viewpoint is more pragmatic and rather legally oriented.

The second case is the case where some financial institutions are linked through substantial stakes, i.e. participations between 20 and 50 per cent[2].
The question that arises here is the following one: "can two companies who are

---

[1]   In this respect it is interesting to refer to the Norwegian case where they distinguish between groups set up by limited companies at the one hand (with a holding structure combining the different "subsidiaries") and mutuals and saving banks (with an intermediate holding) at the other hand.

[2]   It must be emphasized that also a 20% and a 50% participation are to be considered as substantial holdings.

linked via a participation of e.g. 40 per cent be considered as companies of the same group and to which extent has the "owning" company control over the "owned" company ?"

In practice, an equal-or-more-than-20-per cent-participation indicates a lasting relationship between two companies[3]. However we can't make any conclusions about the level of independency of the two companies. On the one hand, a participation of 20 per cent can be sufficient to control a company (distinction is made between formal control - majority of votes - and factual control - a dominant influence); on the other hand, a holding of 40 per cent does not necessarily mean that one can exercise control.

Then, everything depends on the criterion one uses to describe a group: if a lasting relationship is a sufficient condition, one can conclude that with every participation of more than 20 per cent[4] the two companies involved belong to the same group. As mentioned before, this is not always the case if you use control as the appropriate criterion.

This is the point of disagreement between specialists: some opt for the inclusion of these companies as members of the same group, while others argue that this isn't the case.

This discussion has primarily legal rather than economic backgrounds. The opponents put forward that an "owning" company never can exercise control in such an extent than is the case with a majority holding. This will result in practical problems for the "owning" company and supervisory authorities. From this, they conclude that it's better not to consider the two companies as part of the same group.

In our opinion, this discussion disregards the economic reality and therefore, we think that legal considerations (although easier to handle) should not be the only reference point for economic decisions. The economic reality is that we are confronted with the combined offer of financial, insurance and investment products and that this combination has consequences both on business and on the macro economic level. This should be the subject of legislation. The type of the conglomerate should have no influence to that respect because this would rather lead to regulatory arbitrage which should be avoided.

Consequently, we put greather emphasis on the criterion "lasting relationship" than on the criterion "control" and therefore, we argue that participations equal to

---

[3]   The only exception are the "Latin" holding companies, frequently found in Belgium, France, Italy and other "Latin" countries. Between these holding companies and their "daughters", there exists no operational integration ; the holding company rules the roost at the General Meeting and in most of the cases, this company is also represented in the Board of Directors.

[4]   Also a participation of exactly 20% might be sufficient.

or more than 20 per cent should be considered as an indication that two companies belong to the same group. An exception has to be made for holding relations (starting from 20% up to 33%) where no operational integration exists. Additional variables[5] could be of great help to detect if this is the case. This solution is probably also acceptable for the pertinent remarks made by J.H. Holsboer (ING, the Netherlands) and K.W. Knauth (Gesamtverband der Deutschen Versicherungs-wirtschaft e.V., Germany).

The last case considers institutions linked up with minority shares or co-operation agreements.
Most specialists agree that these kind of institutions don't form a group. However, some comments can be put forward against this viewpoint.

> "An alternative and broader concept of financial conglomerate would regard it as an entity which offers to the public a range of services either financial or financial and non-financial together... When they are supplied by a group made up by several companies, those companies are linked through majority holdings or effective control so that joint marketing and mutual responsibilities go together. Where this is not the case the concept of financial conglomeration can still be applied whenever financial products are marketed jointly if risks assumed by a component of the conglomerate indirectly involve the others (EC-DGXV-110/85)".

In this case, also marketing arrangements and joint ventures can lead to a combined offering of financial products, investments, and/or insurance products. Here, we make the same remark as in the former case. We consider companies involved in such a way as conglomerates, on condition that there is some operational integration or some involvement of the risks of the two companies.

An important issue is whether indirect participations also should be taken into account to calculate the total percentage of the participation. In our opinion, this is certainly the case because groups are not always structured in a simple and a flat way. The question remains how far "indirect" relationships should be taken into account. We would suggest to limit this "indirect ownership" to relations in the "third degree" (vertical as well as horizontal). Also the suggestion made by P. Pearson to integrate indirect ownership for those cases where the ownership is mediated by the "way of control" could be an extra reference base.

Again the Latin conglomerates are causing some troubles, but these cases are relatively marginal in the financial sector. Perhaps, some special rules should be provided to solve some specific problems.

---

[5]   Such as the division of votes in the meeting of shareholders, nomination of directors and board members, unity of organization, real influence on the management, marketing joint ventures etc.

9.1.3. DEFINING DIFFERENT KINDS OF FINANCIAL INSTITUTIONS

The second crucial point in the general definition points out that a financial conglomerate should consist of different kinds of financial institutions or of different types of financial services or activities.

Financial institutions can be defined as "enterprises whose assets and liabilities consist almost exclusively of financial instruments (direct and/or indirect financial assets)".

According to this definition, the most relevant categories are:

- financial intermediaries: these financial institutions act as an intermediary between economic agents with financial surpluses and those with financial shortages; a further distinction is made between monetary institutions (banks, savings banks) and non-monetary financial intermediaries (mortgage banks): the first category issues monetary instruments ("payment instruments") while the latter doesn't;
- institutional investors: these financial institutions don't primarily act as financial intermediaries but their core business is to collect money they have to invest. Insurance companies (both life as well as non life insurers) are examples of this category.

There's no clear definition of a financial institution in the EC-directives, but there is an enumeration of possible financial institutions:

- credit institutions: banks, savings banks and institutions specialised in the provision of short, medium or long term debt;
- insurance companies;
- building societies;
- investment companies;
- equivalent institutions (according to historical situations and differences this has to be filled in per country).

However, K.W. Knauth has some problems with this description of a financial institution. According to him (and this is also the German point of view), it would not be correct to describe insurance companies in Europe by the term "financial institutions" because the activity an insurance company performs - the management of risks - cannot be considered as a financial service.

Moreover, their activity can't be put on the same level of banks or investment firms.

Of course, banking is not insuring. Though, market research in Belgium has proved that these activities (together with investing) have a great deal in common in the eyes of the consumer[6]. Especially the "grey" zone between investment, savings and insurance is continuously leading to mixed products which can hardly be distinguished in their banking or insurance character. Moreover, the growing number of alliances between credit institutions, insurance companies and investment institutions has shown that suppliers more and more get convinced of the relation between these different activities.

Therefore, it is logical to consider them as "related financial activities".

We do agree with K.W. Knauth that there remains an important difference between non-life insurance and typical monetary banking products. The relationship here doesn't lay in the products themselves but more in the investment function performed with these funds so that, there again, one can speak of comparable "financial" institutions.

Caused by the lack of a clear definition of a financial institution, the concept of "different kinds of financial institutions" is often translated into "being subject to different types of supervisory rules". Then, a financial conglomerate should comprise financial institutions which are subject to supervision in terms of Community Law, from at least two of the following categories: credit institutions, insurance companies or investment institutions (A. Vermaat - paragraph 2.1.3.). This is also the definition used in the working group on financial conglomerates, set up by the Conference of Insurance Supervisors of the European Community.

According to Mr. Pearson some problems may arise with regard to certain unsupervised (financial) undertakings and certain holding companies. However these problems are on the level of supervision and have nothing to do with the scope of activities which are performed by a financial conglomerate.

Therefore, we can agree with his statement: "It follows that the presence of "supervised undertakings" shall be a necessary condition for the existence of a conglomerate whereas the presence of unsupervised (financial) undertakings or holding companies would just be a possible additional element".

Noteworthy is that financial conglomerates not only contain financial institutions. Sometimes a conglomerate can have considerable participations in commercial and industrial undertakings. This is certainly not a problem if these participations remain subordinate[7] to the financial activities; if however the amount of financial

---

[6]   Prof. dr. L.A.A. Van den Berghe, "Uitbouw van een klantgerichte marketingstrategie voor verzekeringen en financiële produkten - onderzoek naar de optimale assen voor een innovatieve marktsegmentering" (Construction of a client oriented marketing strategy for insurance and financial products - investigation of the optimal axes for an innovative market segmentation), Strategic report, Vlerick School voor Management, 1992-1993.

[7]   In this respect the reference base is often the balance sheet total of the combined activities. A substantial part is then defined as more than 50% of the balance sheet total. Sometimes reference is also made to the turnover (even percentages of 10% are cited in this respect).

services within such a group is relatively small in comparison with the other activities, the supervisory authorities and the European Commission speak of "mixed groups" or "non financial conglomerates". Directive 92/30/EEC distinguishes between "mixed-activity holding companies" and "financial holding companies".

Because of supervisory problems (this group would be so heterogeneous that group supervision would not give a meaningful picture) the first category is not considered to be a financial conglomerate.

From an economic viewpoint once again one can make some remarks. If these conglomerates are excluded from legislation in this respect, the economic reality is distorted.

The "real" financial conglomerates can also be subdivided in different groups: in the Netherlands, there is a distinction between:

-   conglomerates with a primarily insurance character;
-   conglomerates with a primarily banking character;
-   mixed financial conglomerates.

This division is called the "tripartite subdivision" and is based upon the total legally required solvency margin (80 %/20 % boundaries). In se, these conglomerates all have different characteristics and probably meet different problems. Perhaps this is a topic for further research.

9.1.4. APPLYING THE DEFINITIONS IN PRACTICE

Different aspects of the definition were applied on a database that was developed within the EFIC to examine the impact of different definitions on the number and the type of financial conglomerates. Furthermore, we wanted to have a notion of the economic impact of the whole conglomeration movement.

In the first instance, we analysed the impact of different definitions on the number of financial conglomerates in the EU.

For that purpose, we created the concept "Qualified institution"[8], i.e. an insurance institution, a credit institution or a holding company with participations in the other type of financial institutions. In our database, we found 121 qualified institutions in the EU. These 121 institutions belonged to 85 different financial conglomerates.

If we compare those findings with figures from other sources (such as the CEA), we can conclude that the difference between our results and the results of the other

---

[8]   For the exact content of this term, we refer to chapter 3 (3.2.1. Defining the type and number of financial conglomerates).

sources is obvious. Even if we enlarge our sample with the category "possible financial conglomerates"[9] - at this moment we have 101 financial conglomerates - the figures we obtain are significantly smaller than the figures of the others. Partly, this is due to the fact that we used different scopes, but we think another important reason for this difference could be that the definitions of the others aren't always that accurate.

The first purpose of the database was to test the different definitions and to analyse the impact on the number of conglomerates in the EU.
As mentioned above, if we considered the 5 per cent level (i.e. two companies belong to the same group if one has a participation of more than 5 per cent in the other), 121 qualified institutions arose out of the database: 61 insurers, 55 credit institutions and 5 holding companies. The difference between the number of qualified insurance and credit institutions is too small to make obvious conclusions about the division of certain types of conglomerates in the EU.

If we draw up the level of participation from 5 per cent to 20 per cent (a substantial stake), the total number of qualified institutions decreases to 104. It is remarkable that this drop-off is predominantly due to the decrease of insurance companies with participations in credit institutions. This can be seen on the figures below: the differences between the white bars and the grey bars are generally smaller in figure 1 than in figure 2 (see next page).
We thought a possible explanation was the more strategic character of participations of credit institutions in insurance institutions (or mixed holdings); insurance institutions are institutional investors so their participations can have an economic character while this isn't the case for the participations of credit institutions.

However, when we only consider mother/daughter relationships (i.e. participations of 50 per cent and more), the decrease to 82 qualified institutions is predominantly caused by a decrease of credit institutions, rather than by insurance institutions. This can also be deducted from the two figures below: now the differences between the bar indicating the 20 per cent level and the bar of the 50 per cent level are relatively bigger in figure 1.
We have no explicit explanation for that.

---

[9]   Again, we refer to chapter 3 for a more detailed and an accurate description of the term.

Figure 1: Qualified credit institutions - Course at different percentage levels.

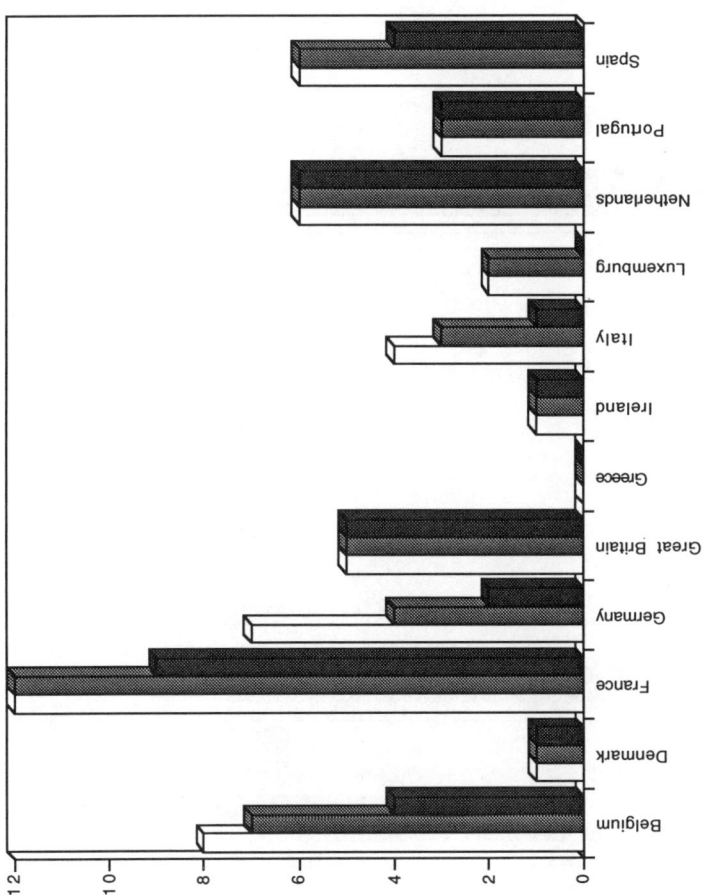

Figure 2: Qualified insurance institutions - Course at different percentage levels.

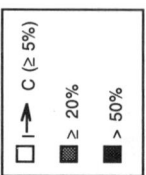

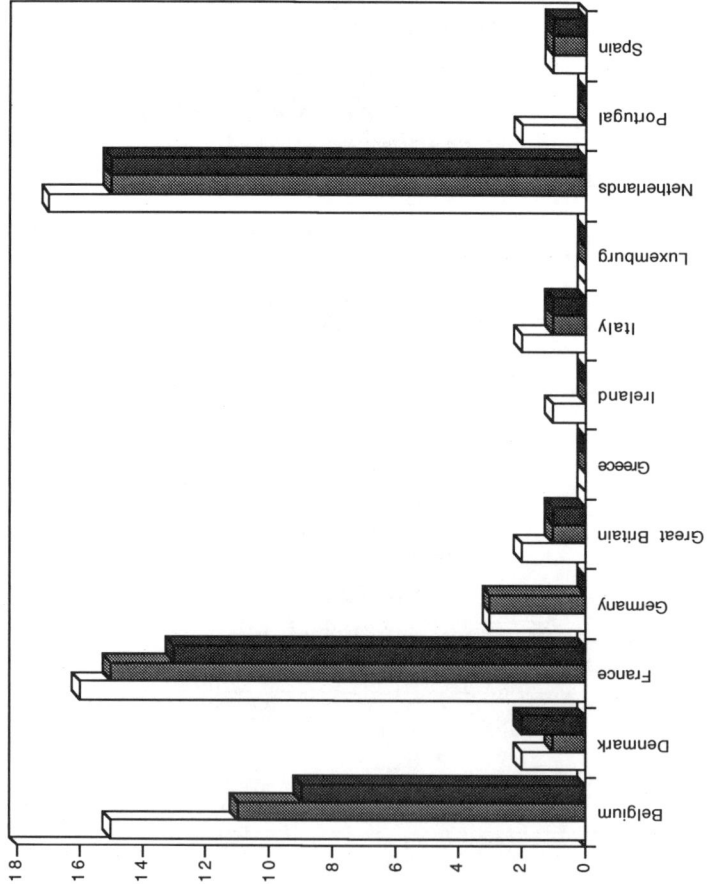

We have also tried to measure the economic impact of these financial groups. In this task we were only partially succesful; therefore, we could only give some estimations.

We had financial data of 77 groups, collected from the consolidated annual reports of 1992[10].

The economic impact of the whole conglomeration movement can be deducted from the companies we have found in our tables. At a glance, we can see that most of the companies that were mentioned here, belong to biggest companies of their respective countries.

The premium income of the financial conglomerates represented 44 per cent of the total premium income in the EU. However, this 44 per cent is only an approximation of the real figure because some corrections should be made.

Again, we made a subdivision between conglomerates with a primarily insurance character, conglomerates with a primarily banking character and mixed holdings, i.e. mother companies of groups with almost equal parts of insurance and "banking" activities. Thereby, we used some key figures, such as total income (i.e. the sum of premium income, interest income and other operating income), balance sheet total and the number of employees.

It is important to notice that according to the criterion we used, the lists of the sorted companies differed significantly.

If we sorted the conglomerates by total income (see table 3.6), the list was headed by three insurance groups (Allianz, AXA and UAP), followed by three banking groups (Crédit Lyonnais, Deutsche Bank and Crédit Agricole) and the Dutch mixed group ING. It was also remarkable that the lion's share of the first ranked companies consisted of companies of Germany and France.

On the contrary, if we took the total number of employees as the sorting criterion (see table 3.8), it were two British banks who were heading the list: Barclays Bank and National Westminster. Strange because they were not mentioned in the top 20 classified by total income or balance sheet total.

If we sorted on balance sheet total, we found 13 credit institutions in the top 15. The list was headed by Crédit Lyonnais, Deutsche Bank, Crédit Agricole and Banque Nationale de Paris.

The dominance of credit institutions in the top 20 of the balance sheet total and the number of employees can partly be explained by specific characteristics of their business activities:

---

[10] Remember the 85 (or 101 potential) financial conglomerates we had found in the database.

- bank products are distributed by the bank's employees, while an important part of the insurance products are distributed through independent agents and brokers;
- the balance sheet total of banks is comparatively more "voluminous" than the one of insurance companies, because it contains all monetary transactions with clients as well as in relation to inter-bank funding; the off-balance sheet evolution is certainly decreasing this difference.

Therefore, we conclude that it is dangerous to split up financial conglomerates in insurance conglomerates, credit conglomerates and mixed financial conglomerates on the base of only these criterions. Some other criterions should also be involved to distinguish between these three categories. However, more research is needed to be able to give a concrete interpretation for this.

9.2. PART II - REGULATING FINANCIAL CONGLOMERATES

9.2.1. RISKS IN RELATION TO FINANCIAL CONGLOMERATES

The integration of different kinds of financial institutions into financial conglomerates leads to new organisational and financial structures for the institutions concerned. Changes in the perceived risks - especially relevant for the supervisory authorities are the result. This concerns:

- the risk of instability and the insolvency risk (the risk of double gearing, the increased total business risk and the risk of contagion);
- the risk of non-transparency (the risk of regulatory arbritage, the risk of the metamorphose effect and the risk of opaque structures);
- the risk of infringing the free competition and the rights of the consumer (the risk of decreasing competition and abuse of power and the risk of conflicts of interest).

It is clear that preventive measures should be taken to cope with these potential risks. However, until now there is not a divergence of view on how to cope with the monitoring of these risks. Against the background of the different views held it should be mentioned that especially the financial risks should not be overestimated. Integration of different kinds of business also does have a positive, risk-spreading effect.

Also the risk of decreasing competition should not be overestimated in the light of the disappearance of geographical boundaries within the E.C.

9.2.2. SUPERVISION OF FINANCIAL CONGLOMERATES

Most supervisory systems were until recently structured in view of the traditional boundaries between banks, insurance companies and investment firms. The Netherlands give one of the leading examples on a national level of how the supervision of financial conglomerates can be structured by co-operation of the banking and the insurance supervisor. On an international level the B.C.C.I.-directive was the first official step in the direction of co-ordinating the supervision of financial conglomerates. By this directive rules are given concerning the transparency of financial groups, the "suitability" of major shareholders and managers of financial groups, the circumvention of the risk of arbitrage and the exchange of information between different types of supervisory authorities. The further crystallization of these rules and of rules concerning accounting and consolidation matters, the protection of consumers, the prevention of double gearing and the responsibility for the supervision are still under discussion.

9.2.3. SOLVENCY REGULATIONS FOR FINANCIAL CONGLOMERATES

For the moment, no specific requirements exist in relation to the solvency of financial conglomerates. So, special attention was paid to the comparison of the solvency regulations for banks and insurance companies. A distinction was made between the prescribed methods to calculate the required level of the solvency margin and the rules concerning the admittance of the components that constitute the solvency fund available.

The required solvency level for banks is based on the determination of a so-called risk based capital ratio. This risk based capital ratio replaced the former capital-to-assets ratio to take account of increasing debt risks resulting from the Third World debt-crisis, increasing risks resulting from the introduction of off-balance sheet instruments and (the recognition of) the risks inherent in "large exposures".

The solvency rules for the insurance sector are completely different from the rules for the banking sector. Within the rules for insurance companies a distinction is made between life and non-life companies.
For life insurance companies the required solvency margin is primarily based on the amount of the technical provisions and the amount of the capital under risk. For non-life insurance companies a calculation based on the "average claims due" and a calculation based on the "premium volume" has to be made. The highest of the resulting amounts ultimately determines the required solvency margin. The risk-decreasing effect of reinsurance is to a certain extent taken into account by the application of reduction factors.

Also the rules concerning the admittance of components of the solvency fund are different for banks and insurance companies although the differences decreased since the third EC-directives became into force.

The solvency fund of banks consists of tier 1 components (taken into account for their total value) and tier 2 components of lower quality (taken into account for 50 or 25 % of their value).

Within the rules for insurance companies again a distinction is made between life and non-life companies. Hidden reserves (life and non-life) and future profits (life) can eventually be taken into account.

For credit institutions also a deposit insurance system is required. For insurance companies requirements concerning different kinds of technical provisions complement the solvency requirements.

The philosophy behind the EU-solvency regulation is at the micro and the market level quite similar for banks and for insurance companies. In both cases the aim is to protect the financial interests of the clients and to facilitate free competition. At the macro-level the monetary function plays a major role in the supervision of banks; in the supervision of insurance companies this element is not a major point of interest.

Because of the nature of the business involved solvency rules for banks are focused on asset risks, while solvency rules for insurance companies are focused on liability risks, although for life insurers also asset risks are taken into account. At last should be mentioned that banks are supervised on an institutional level, while insurance companies are supervised on a company level.

9.2.4. THE POSSIBILITY OF A GLOBAL APPROACH FOR THE CALCULATION OF THE SOLVENCY REQUIREMENTS OF FINANCIAL CONGLOMERATES

Due to differences in activities, accounting principles, legal requirements, etc. it is not easy to develop a common measure for all risks involved. Simply stating that solvency margins have to be added isn't a sufficient solution from a conceptual perspective. The results of some simulation exercises to compare the levels of the solvency requirements for banks and insurance companies were presented. Because the measures used for insurance companies cannot be applied to banks, the simulations made concern the application of the banking rules to insurance companies. Some assumptions had to be made in respect to the categorisation of creditors and countries and the use of off-balance sheet transactions.

Analysis of the solvency funds of especially the life insurers taken into account shows that revaluation reserves constitute a relatively large part of the solvency fund. However based on the banking rules the admittance of such reserves is limited. For this reason one of the four companies studied didn't have a really substantial solvency surplus and was confronted with a higher solvency margin required on the basis of the banking rules.

Due to differences in investment policy the weighted assets-method results in lower solvency requirements for non-life companies as for life companies. However from an insurance perspective the non-life business is far more risky than the life business. So the banking rules are not very useful for non-life companies.

The banking rules also misstate the risk of larger companies by only taking into account the greater risk of a more sophisticated investment policy (resulting in the selection of riskier assets). The risk reducing effect of diversification (investment risk) and the law of large numbers (underwriting risk) is overlooked.

By not taking into account the effect of inflation, the minimum solvency requirements have become "outdated". Taking into account the "EU-inflation" leads to a correction of more than three times the current level for the non-life branches and of more than two times for the life branches. Due to the more recent origin of the banking solvency minima, only minor changes result for the banking sector.

9.2.5. DISCUSSION ON RISKS AND SOLVENCY

In Norway one set of requirements is applicable for credit institutions, insurance and holding companies consisting of one set of rules that apply to the credit risk and one set of that apply to the insurance risk. The philosophy used is that the credit risk attached to investments is the same for all kinds of financial institutions. Underwriting risk is unique for insurance companies.
Because also the EC-requirements are implemented now, Norway will have a two track system. However calculations show that once the Norwegian rules are satisfied, virtually all the EC-requirements will be satisfied too.
In Norway the capital adequacy rules are also applied on a consolidated basis.
The basis of uniform rules for banks and insurance companies will result in a "reshuffling" of credit risks within a group resulting in lower capital requirements for some given overall level of risk.

In the U.S.A. the NAIC also has recently developed a system of risk-based capital requirements for insurance companies. For life insurers the asset-default risk, the insurance risk and the interest risk while for non-life insurers the asset risk, the credit risk, the loss reserve risk and the written premium risk are taken into account. These new rules already have a notable effect on the risk behaviour of insurers.

The solo-plus approach to supervision secures a strict protection between the legal entities of the individual companies, giving a guarantee for the client to prevent contagion. Consolidated supervision by the banking supervision can well lead to conflicts of interests in the case the supervisor also has monetary responsibilities. At last differences in the existing approaches for the supervision of banks (basically material and pro-active) and of insurance companies (basically normative and retro-active) make a consolidated approach difficult.

The fact that credit risks depend on economic factors makes the point of double gearing more serious for banks than for insurance companies. The value of shares held in other banks will also be correlated with the same economic factors.

9.3.   PART III - STRATEGIC ISSUES

9.3.1. STRATEGIC ISSUES

The synergies of forming a financial conglomerate can potentially be found in the realisation of economies of scale and/or of scope. The thesis that the formation of certain types of financial conglomerates can be seen as an application of the new strategic thinking of "stretch and leverage " was developed. New management ideas are based on the view that it is not the strategic fit but the strategic gap that counts for the creative and inventive development of a company. In fact the Schumpeterian entrepreneur is back in the picture as the central force to build upon "core competencies".

However especially within the financial service sector the importance of the support and co-operation of everybody within the organisation must not be ignored. So the classical "tools" will still play an important role in the implementation of the strategic intentions based on the new insights. Nevertheless because the most ambitious strategies answer to the most modern management recipes, new risks will come forth. If those risks will not be tackled it could be that ambitious strategic gaps will prove to be far too large to be bridged.

9.3.2. BASIS STATEMENTS TO BE TESTED IN FURTHER RESEARCH

- Financial conglomerates are far too heterogeneous globally as well as individually, to consider them as a single concept on which a straightforward structure (definition, typology) and strategy can be applied. it is therefore better to speak of the (movement of financial conglomeration) instead of referring to financial conglomerates.
- The successes and failures are more easy to define in theory than they can be handled in practice. This has to do with the complex set of determining factors, that need to be studied further before any suggestion can be made of how and why to set up a financial conglomerate. It is consequently very dangerous to

copy successes of other firms or of other countries, without taking into account these specific determining factors. The danger of copying strategies and of defensive moves may not be overestimated.

Preliminary research results show a significant influence of the following strategic choices:

* degree of legal integration (type of market entry and dynamic adaptations);
* degree of operational and functional integration[11] (marketing, distribution, funding, know how and staff members, information technology, etc.);
* degree of product integration[12];
* degree of complementarity between the portfolio of clients, products, marketing and production techniques;
* number of experiences, type and duration of experience.

- Although management literature and consultants mostly proclaim that structure follows strategy, it is often so that in practice, the structure sets the limits to the potential strategies.

Diminishing the structural limitations, replacing the boundaries of the own branch and regulations will permit that a more optimal strategic approach becomes feasible. Stretch and leverage strategies based on core competences lead to better results.

Index

A

abuse of power 71, 72
active company 59
asset risks 86, 113
asset-restrictions 74

B

balance sheet total 62, 64, 66, 68
balance sheets 65
blurring of the boundaries 107, 108
blurring of the traditional boundaries 73
business risk 69
business strategy 151

C

capital adequacy requirements 47
capital adequacy rules 37
capital under risk 79
Chinese walls 76
close links 32
co-operation 55
common ownership 19
complementarity 2, 12, 14
complementary 14, 18
complementary activity 13
complementary financial services 12
complete consolidation 75
concentric diversification 14
concerns 24
conflicts of interest 72, 76, 139
conglomerate 21, 22, 24
conglomerate diversification 14
conglomerates with a primarily banking
     character 62, 167
conglomerates with a primarily insurance
     character 62, 167
consolidated supervision 139
consolidation 74, 127
consolidation methods 4
consolidation of holdings 46

control 3, 6, 32, 159
control criterion 6
core capital 92
core competence 151
country of the creditor 78, 90
credit conglomerates 64
credit conversion degree 79
credit holding 54
credit risk 78, 90, 125
criteria of fitness and properness 74
cross-selling 75
cross-subsidisation 129
cyclical risks 84

D

dependent company 7
deposit insurance mechanism 83
deposit insurance system 83
direct 3, 5
direct or indirect ownership 26
direct ownership of capital or voting rights
     32
direct participations 5
discussion Holsboer 139
discussion Knauth 142
discussion Løining 128
discussion Pearson 145
discussion Simonsen 125
diversification 14
double gearing 30, 69, 70, 75, 111,
     127, 129, 143
downstream 74
droit de suite 26, 27

E

economic 3
economic group 24
economies of scale 149
economies of scale and scope 108
economies of scope 149, 150
effective control 7, 18, 19, 26

egalisation reserve 84, 87
embedded value 82
employee 68
    balance sheet total
        total income 67
exchange risk 90

F

factual control 7, 159
financial conglomerate holding company
    35
financial conglomerates in the broadest
    sense 9
financial conglomerates in the strict sense
    9
financial conglomerates without any
    economic integ 9
financial group 34, 38, 47
financial institution 2, 9, 10, 11, 28,
    29, 36, 37, 43, 48, 54, 161
financial institutions 161
financial instruments 9
financial intermediary 85
financial markets 9
financial services or activities 2
fire walls 40
fit and proper criteria 73
formal control 159
formal legal control 7
FORTIS case 153

G

general conglomerate 23
group 2, 6, 12, 16, 18, 19, 24, 30,
    31, 35, 38, 54, 158
group company 16
groups with a predominantly financial
    character 12
groups with a predominantly insurance
    character 12

H

hidden reserves 82, 83
holding 2, 54

holding company 39
holdings in financial institutions 43
home country control 84
homogeneous financial institutions 12
horizontal diversification 14
horizontal integration 73

I

IBNR reserve 84
indirect ownership 32, 160
indirect participations 3, 5
industrial conglomerate 21, 22
influence 4
ING-Group 154
insurance conglomerates 64
insurance financial conglomerates 24
insurance holding 54
insurance risk 86, 107, 125
integration 7
interest risk 90
interlocking directorship 72
intragroup transactions 129
investment 3, 4, 28
investment financial conglomerates 24
investment risk 107, 109, 113, 121

L

large exposures 79
large risk 79, 91
lasting relationship 4, 159
legal control 7
legal integration 3, 9
lender of the last resort 85
level of solvency 86
level playing field 26
levels of participation 5
liability risk 79, 80, 86
liability-restrictions 74

M

majority holdings 18, 19, 158
majority participations 61
maximum ownership 37
measure of control 7

metamorphose effect 71
minimum level of solvency 80, 89, 91, 97
minimum solvency 108
minimum solvency margin 146
minimum solvency requirements 113
minor stake 5, 59
mixed financial conglomerates 12, 23, 24
mixed group 27, 29, 34, 37, 39, 47
mixed holding 55, 62, 64
mixed holdings 167
mixed-activity groups 34
models financial conglomerate 8
mother/daughter relationship 5, 59

N

NAIC 132, 133
non-financial conglomerates 24
non-financial holdings 55
non-transparant 74
non-transparency 71
not primarily financial conglomerate 23
number of employees 62, 65, 66

O

OBS 111
OBS activities 90
off-balance instruments 87
off-balance sheet transactions 78, 111
off-balance-sheet elements 91
opaque structures 71, 73
operational integration 9
ownership 3, 4, 6
ownership limitations 39

P

parent undertaking 31
participation 3, 4, 17, 26, 32, 55, 56, 58, 59, 60
passive company 59
primarily banking (credit/securities) financial co 24
primarily banking financial conglomerates 23

primarily insurance financial conglomerates 23
Protocol 73, 139
protocol 23

Q

qualified holding 3
qualified institution 56, 59, 60, 61, 163
qualifying holdings 3

R

range of activities 74
regulatory arbitrage 71, 157
relationship between the undertakings 31
required level of solvency 77, 78
required solvency level 169
required solvency margin 169
restrictions on voting rights 45
risk assets ratio 78, 79
risk based capital 141
risk of contagion 70, 142
risk-assets ratio 78
risk-based capital 133, 140, 171
risk-spreading 70
risks business 27
rules of consolidation 51

S

significant influence 3, 17
single licence 84
solidity requirements 125, 126
solo-plus 26, 139
solo-plus approach 171
solo-plus supervision 139
solo-plus system 76
solvency fund 77, 81, 87, 169
solvency funds 170
solvency margin 79, 101, 102, 103
solvency regulations 77, 85
solvency requirements 79, 80, 107
specialised financial conglomerates 24
strategic issues 149
stretch and leverage 150

subordinated loans 82, 111, 131
subsidiaries 17
subsidiary 31
substantial stake 5, 59, 164
substantial stakes 158
supervised undertakings 33
supervision 72
supervision of financial conglo-merates
    76
Supervision of financial conglomerates
    169
synergies 14, 149

T

technical provisions 84, 108
the risk of decreasing competition 71
third generation directives 85
tier 1 81, 84, 92
tier 2 81, 92
total income 62, 63, 66
transactions between enterprises in a
    financial gr 41, 50
transparancy 74
two track system 126, 171
two-track solvency requirement 130
type of creditor 78, 90
types of countries 110
types of creditors 110
types of supervisory rules 2

U

undertakings 33
underwriting risk 80, 108, 129
unit linked 113
unit-linked insurance 101
unsupervised (financial) undertakings 33
upfront costs 82
upstream 74

V

vertical division of activities 72
voting power 26
voting rights 3, 4, 26

W

weighted assets 90

Z

Zillmerisation 83
zone A 78
zone B 78

Bibliographic references

Albanese, M.L. & Mayewski, L.G. & McKenna, M. [1994]: "RBC: Beauty contest or non-event?" in Life/Health Best's Review, March, pp. 33-36, 86-88.

Albanese, M.L. & Mayewski, L.G. [1992]: "Risk-Based Capital: Is your company ready?" in Life/Health Best's Review, May, pp. 12, 14, 93-96.

Anonymous [1992]: "RBC technical overview" in Life/Health Best's Review, May, pp. 14, 90-93.

Anonymous [1994]: "A technical overview of RBC" in Property/Casualty Best's Review, February, pp. 98-100.

Anonymous [1994]: "BCAR technical overview" in Life/Health Best's Review, March, pp. 89- 92.

Ansoff, H.I. [1965]: "Corporate strategy", New York.

Ansoff, H.I. [1968]: "Corporate strategy: an analytic approach to business policy for growth and expansion", Harmondsworth, Pinguin Books.

Badon Ghijben, W. [1994]: "Indeling geconsolideerde jaarrekening", Euroforum, Hoofddorp, January 19th-21st.

Bank of England [1993]: "Banking act report for 1992/93", pp. 22-23.

Bank of England: banking supervision division [1992]: " Capital adequacy return (form bsd1)", pp. 5-6.

Bank of England: banking supervision division [1993]: "Notice to institutions authorised under the banking act 1987", pp. 1-4.

BCCI-Directive [1993]: Proposal for a council directive amending the directives of the credit institutions, the insurance companies and the investment firms; com (93), 363 July 29th.

Benink, H.A. [1993]: "Financial integration in Europe", Dordrecht, Kluwer.

Börner, W.H. [1993]: "Die Überwachung der Finanzkonglomerate aus der Sicht eines Deutschen Versicherer", Conference Papers CAPA/EFMA, pp. 267-288.

Brittan, L.[1991]: European Commission, November 4th.

BS (Belgisch Staatsblad) [1990]: "Hoofdstuk 10: Koninklijk Besluit van 6 maart 1990 op de geconsolideerde jaarrekening van de ondernemingen (officieuze coördinatie)", March 27th.

Burgert, R. & Timmermans, C.W.A & Joosten, H.F.J. [1990]: "Jaarrekening nieuwe stijl deel 2", Samson H.D. Tjeenk Willink.

C.E.A. [1993]: "Financial conglomerates - conglomerats financiers", Comité Européen des Assurances, Special Issue, n° 2, July, pp. 2-4.

CDV [1992-93]: "Annual report of the insurance supervisor in Belgium", pp. 77.

Central Bank of Ireland [1992]: "Annual Report".

Chandler, A. [1962]: "Strategy and structure: chapters in the history of American industrial enterprise", Cambridge.

Clarotti, P. [1992]: "The EC Commission view on the supervision of financial conglomerates", CEPS-seminar, Brussels, December.

Commissie voor Bank en Financiewezen [1993]: "Jaarverslag 1992/1993", pp. 121-123.

Coopers & Lybrand [1993]: "Making bancassurance work: survey of European financial institutions' policies and practice", pp. 31, Coopers & Lybrand, European Financial Services Group, Amsterdam.

Cousy, H. [1992]: "Algemene inleiding en eigenheid van bank- en verzekerings-activiteit: relatie met cliënten, een juridische benadering", Achtste Leuvense Verzekeringsdagen, May 22nd and 23rd.

Covalsky, J.M. [1994]: "After dumping properties carriers await RBC filing" in Life/Health Best's Review, January, pp. 42-44.

De Nederlandsche Bank [1992]: "Annual Report 1992".

De Verzekeringswereld [1993]: "Mislukking of succes? De a posteriori controle", pp. 41, October 18th.

Dickinson, G. & Dinensis, E. [1993]: " The changing interface between insurance companies and banks", 20th Seminar Geneva Association, Rotterdam, September.

Douma, S.W. [1990]: "Concernstrategie" in Bedrijfskunde, volume 62, n°2, pp.120-128.

European Insurance Market [1994]: "The supervision of financial conglomerates", issue n° 54, pp. 132-134.

FEE (Fédération des Experts comptables Européens) [1994]: "Report of the FEE task force on financial conglomerates to the European Commission : The form and content of the consolidated financial statements of financial conglomerates".

Financieele Dagblad, [1994]: "ING-bestuurder kritiseert concept EU-Richtlijn", March 17th.

Fitchew, G.E. [1992]: "A global approach to financial services - The EC Commission's point of view", CEA, Londen, October 15th.

Forestieri, G. [1993]: "Economies of scale and scope in the financial services industry: a review of recent literature" in Financial Market Trends, n° 4, pp. 63-123, October.

Gardener, E.P.M. [1987b]: "Strategic challenges for banks in Europe" in European Management Journal, Volume 5, n° 4.

Gardener, E.P.M. [1987]: "Structural and strategic consequences of financial conglomeration" in Bank-& Financiewezen/Revue de la Banque, n° 9, pp. 5-15, Brussels.

Goldfinger, C. [1986]: "La géofinance - pour comprendre la mutation financière", Collection Odysée - Editions du Seuil, Paris.

Goode (Ed.) R.M. [1986]: "Conflicts of interest in the changing financial world", Institute of bankers, London.

Hamel, G. & Prahalad, C.K. [1993]: "Strategy as stretch and leverage", in Harvard Business Review, March-April.

Herring, R.J. & Santomero, A.M. [1990]: "The corporate structure of financial conglomerates" in Journal of Financial Services Research, pp. 471-497.

Hesberg, D. & Karten, W. [1994]: "Supervision of financial conglomerates - remarks on solvency control and alleged double gearing", Geneva Papers on Risk and Insurance, pp. 1-21.

Holsboer, J.H. [1993]: "Specialization and diversification in financial services" in Geneva Papers on Risk and Insurance, Issues & Practices, n° 69, pp. 388-398.

Ingham, H. & Thompson, S. [1994]: "Whole-owned vs. collaborative ventures for diversifying financial services" in Strategic Management Journal, Volume 15, pp. 325-334.

IOSCO (International Organisation Of Securities Commissions) [1992]: "Principles for the supervision of financial conglomerates".

Kazuya Mizushima [1989]: "Allfinanzstreben gefährdet Identität der Versicherung" in Versicherungswirtschaft, n° 17, pp. 1156 - 1161, Japan.

Kellogg, P.B. & Simpson, E.M. [1994]: "NAIC's RBC: a virtual reality" in Property/Casualty Best's Review, February 1994, pp. 49-51, 54, 88-99.

Kerns, Chr. & Reed, S. [1994]: "Significant insurance ruling from the NAIC; US insurance commissioners make risk based capital standards mandatory for property casualty insurers" in Lloyd's List, September.

Kessler, D. [1989]: "L'evolution des relations entre banques et assurances" in Etudes et Dossiers, n° 141, pp. 3 - 15, Geneva Association, General Assembly, Paris, June 5th.

Koguchi, K. [1993]: "Financial conglomeration" in Financial Market Trends, n° 4, pp. 7-62, October.

Kotler, P. [1994]: "Marketing management: analysis, planning, implementation, and control", Prentice-Hall International.

Kredietbank Weekberichten [1994]: "Problemen met de geconsolideerde jaarrekening in België", volume 49, n°.30, pp.1-7, November 4th

Kroll & Tract [1994]: "NAIC adds risk-based capital rules to state accredition package" in Insurance Report, September, pp. 3.

Leemreis, A.R. [1994]: "De interne verzekeringsmarkt van de Europese Gemeenschap en het Nederlandse belastingrecht", Conference April 29th, Vereniging voor Verzekeringswetenschap.

Loma [1994]: "Risk-Based Capital in the life insurance industry", Georgia.

Maycock, J. [1986]: "Financial conglomerates", Gower Studies in Finance and Investment, University Press Cambridge.

Mogg, J.F. [1993]: "Financial conglomerates", Presentation to the CEA annual common market committee meeting Brussels, September 30th.

Moret & Limperg [1994]: "Het nieuwe jaarrekeningenrecht", Rotterdam.

Moret Ernst & Young [1993]: "Financiële verslaggeving van bancassurance concerns", May, pp. 5-6, 17-25, The Hague.

Morgan, G. & Sturdy, A. & Daniel, J. & Knights, D. [1994]: "Bancassurance in Britain and France: Innovating Strategies in the Financial Services" in The Geneva Papers on Risk and Insurance, 19 (n°. 71, April), pp. 178-195.

OECD [1993]: "Special features - financial conglomerates", OECD Financial Affairs Division.

OJEC L 29, [1992]: directive 92/121/EC - large risks directive.

OJEC L 110, [1992]: directive 92/30/EC - consolidation of credit institutions.

OJEC L 141, [1993]: directive 93/22/EC - investment service directive.

OJEC L 193, [1983]: directive 83/349/EC - seventh directive on accounting principles.

OJEC L 193, [1983]: directive 83/350/EC - the supervision of credit institutions on a consolidated basis.

OJEC L 222, [1978]: directive 78/660/EC - fourth directive on accounting principles.

OJEC L 225/6 [1990]: directive 90/435/EC.

OJEC L 228, [1992]: directive 92/49/EC - third non-life directive.

OJEC L 322, [1977]: directive 77/780/EC - first council directive on the coordination of credit institutions.

OJEC L 332, [1986]: directive 86/566/EC - liberalisation of capital movements.

OJEC L 360, [1992]: directive 92/96/EC - third life directive.

OJEC L 386, [1989]: directive 89/646/EC - second banking directive.

Oosenbrug, A. [1994a]: "De wereld verging; Wie leven d'Or?", inaugural lecture at the Erasmus University Rotterdam on February 4th, Gouda Quint B.V., Arnhem.

Oosenbrug, A. [1994b]: "Life assurer and company tax: technical provisions for life assurers and fiscal profit determination in The Netherlands", The European Accounting Review, pp. 381-384, 3 February.

Ophof, H.P.J. [1992/93]: "Syllabus financieringsrecht", Part II, pp. 79, 83 & 85-86, Rotterdam, Stichting Syllabi.

Pearson, P. [1991]: "Legal aspects of change", ref: PP/yv/67-91.

Pearson, P. [1992]: "Legal aspects of change", Insurance Division, European Community Commission, Brussels.

Pearson, P. [1994]: "The supervision of financial conglomerates: the approach of the European Community", Centre for European Policy Studies, Brussels, March 15th.

Porter, M.E. (Ed.) [1986]: "Competition in global industries", Harvard Business School Press, Boston.

Porter, M.E. [1988]: "From competitive advantage to corporate strategy" in Harvard Business Review, pp. 43-59, May-June.

Porter, M.E. [1991]: "Towards a dynamic theory of strategy" in Strategic Management Journal, pp. 115.

Protocol of May 3rd, 1994, De Nederlandsche Bank & De Verzekeringskamer

Protocol of September 14th, 1990, De Nederlandsche Bank & De Verzekeringskamer.

Report of the working group set up by the Conference of Insurance Supervisors of the European Economic Community with regard to financial conglomerates [1992].

Robens, H. [1987]: "Ursachen und Folgen des Wandels der Wachstumstrategie bei den Anbietern Finanzieller Dienstleistungen" in Versicherungswirtschaft, n° 2, pp. 106-112.

Roos, J. [1994]: "Solvabiliteitseisen voor financiële instellingen binnen de Europese Unie: vergelijkend onderzoek tussen verzekeringsmaatschappijen, beleggingsinstellingen en banken", thesis Erasmus Universiteit, Rotterdam.

Schneider, U.H. [1990]: "Das Aufsichtsrecht der Allfinanz-Konzerne", in Zeitschrift für Wirtschafts- und Bankrecht, volume 44, October 6th, pp. 1649-1692.

Schneider, U.H. [1990]: "Die rechtlichen Rahmenbedingungen der Allfinanz", Sonderdruck aus: Kredit und Kapital, Heft II, Duncker & Humblot, Berlin.

Scholtens, L.J.R. [1993]: "Concentratie in het Nederlandse bank- en verzekeringswezen en de reactie van de toezichthouders" in Maandschrift Economie, volume 57, pp. 466-494.

SVV (Stichting Vakontwikkeling Verzekeringsbedrijf) [1988]: "Verzekeringsleer 1: Het verzekeringsbedrijf, zijn kernfuncties en taakuitoefening", Utrecht.

Van den Berghe, L. & De Waal, L. [1987]: "Strategische beleidsvorming" in Economie van het Verzekeringsbedrijf, pp. 23-32, Kluwer.

Van den Berghe, L. [1981]: "Kritisch onderzoek naar de validiteit van de nationale boekhouding voor de evaluatie van de dienstverlening door de verzekeringssector", Doctoral thesis, R.U.G., Ghent.

Van den Berghe, L. [1983]: "Bank- en financiewezen", Administratieve & Economische Hogeschool, Brussels.

Van den Berghe, L. [1989]: "All-round financiële dienstverlening: een troef of een handicap", research surveys Vlerickschool voor Management, Universiteit Gent.

Van den Berghe, L. [1993]: "Uitbouw van een klantgerichte marketingstrategie voor verzekeringen en financiële produkten - onderzoek naar de optimale assen voor een innovatieve marktsegmentering", Strategic report, pp. 88, Vlerick School voor Management, Ghent.

Van den Berghe, L. [1994a]: "Financial conglomerates: opportunity or threat", Festgabe W. Karten, Hamburg.

Van den Berghe, L. [1994b]: "Financiële conglomeraten" in L.A.A. Van den Berghe, R. Kaas, H. Wolthuis & A. Oosenbrug (Ed.), Erasmus Insurance Centre/ Instituut voor Actuariële Wetenschappen en Econometrie, Rotterdam/Amsterdam.

Van Hulle, K.[1992]: "Consolidatie bij verzekerbanken", Achtste Leuvense Verzekeringsdagen, May 22nd and 23rd.

Verweire, K. [1993]: "Market research and statistical tools to segment the consumer markets for financial services: the case of the Belgian market" in Proceedings of the 20th Seminar of the Group of Risk and Insurance Economists, Geneva Association, pp. 21, Rotterdam.

Verzekeringskamer [1992]: "Supervision of conglomerates, Advantages and disadvantages of 'consolidated' and 'solo-plus' supervision", Apeldoorn.

Verzekeringskamer [1993]: " An analyses of 'solo-plus' supervision", Apeldoorn.

Voorst Vader, V. [1994]: "Het assurantie-intermediair in Nederland - Positie en economische belang, mede gezien in europees perspectief", Conference April 29th, Vereniging voor Verzekeringswetenschap.

Winkler, E.G. [1994]: "Anhörung zur Banken- und Versicherungsmacht", in Versicherungswirtschaft, Heft 2, pp. 132-133.

Working Paper EC "Financial supermarkets", DG XV (specialised services) - 110/85.

Wytzes, H.C. [1978]: "Financiële instellingen en markten", H.E. Stenfert Kroese BV, Leiden.